THE STEP BY STEP ART OF

Origami

THE STEP BY STEP ART OF

Origami

JON TREMAINE

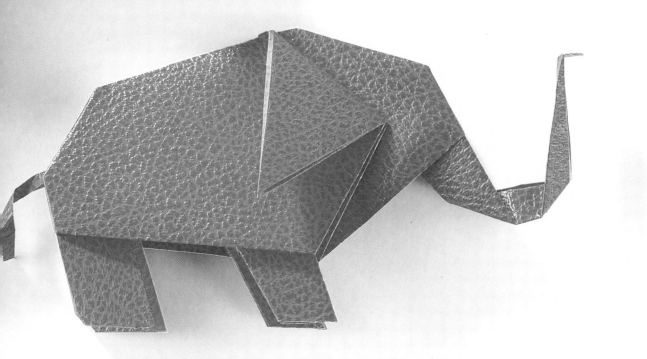

COOMBE BOOKS

For my dear wife, Suzy

4904
This edition published in 1997 by Coombe Books
© 1995 CLB International, Godalming, Surrey, UK
All rights reserved
Printed and bound in Singapore by Tien Wah Press
ISBN 1-85833-709-7

Publisher's Acknowledgement
The publisher would like to thank Staks Ltd,
31 Thames Street, Kingston-upon-Thames,
KT1 1PH for providing properties for
photography on pages 42, 43, 45.

Contents

Introduction
page 10

Techniques
page 12

Crafty Origami
pages 24–31

Table Talk
pages 32–47

Container Crazy
pages 48–65

Clever Creatures
pages 66–79

Festive Flair
pages 80–93

Paper Play
pages 94–105

Diagrams and Templates
pages 106–107

Addresses & Credits
page 108

Introduction

The Art of Origami

When an artist learns his trade, he must always go back to traditional basics. An architect must learn the fundamental principles of building. Only when he has a thorough knowledge of these principles can he create new buildings. A pianist has to practise his scales in order to reach the uncharted heights of musical perfection. So it is with origami.

Have you ever made something out of nothing? Origamaniacs do it all the time! Surely, if you make something out of nothing you must be a magician.

Origamaniacs are magicians.

Origami is Magic.

The Magic of Paper.

The art of origami is to fold a recognizable object from a piece of paper (usually square). With a fold here, a tuck there, the paper folder can create a most delicate flower – or an aggressive animal. A novelty jumping frog – or an elegant swan. An elegant bunch of lilies – or a mammoth herd of elephants.

The traditionalists arrived at their beautiful creations by trial and error. These days computers are used to discover new models. I personally feel that most of the new models have no heart. There is something special about a model that has been created purely by moulding with your hands alone.

Incidently, I left an origami convention late one evening recently *with the remaining delegates sitting in rows with their shoes and socks off, competing with each other to see who could fold the most realistic swan using only their **feet**!*

The most famous paper folder of our times was the late Robert Harbin. I was honoured to count him as a personal friend. We first met 39 years ago. The common bond was through our mutual profession, magic. The meeting place was the headquarters of the illustrious Magic Circle in London. Over a period of many years he personally taught me countless folds. I kept copious records of these folds and now that I have the opportunity to publish a book these notes have proven invaluable.

He had great respect for the work of Kunihiko Kasahara, Isao Honda, Robert Neale, Florence Temko, Ligia Monyoya, John Nordquist, Adolfo Cerceda, Neale Elias, Fred Rohm and George Rhoads, all pioneers of the modern movement. However, nearly all the folds contained in this book are traditional folds; those that have been handed down from father to son, mother to daughter since time immemorial. I have included a few of my original folds to show you how the art can be developed.

I wish you luck with your folding. Keep your points 'pointed' and your creases sharp and you won't go far wrong.

10

Paper

Almost any paper will do! Japanese origami paper is best but giftwrap, paper bags, envelopes with interesting linings, writing paper, computer paper, any paper will do as long as it is not too thick, takes a crease well, and does not easily split when you fold and refold it. Many types of Japanese origami paper are produced. The most common is generally coloured on one side and either white or an entirely different colour on the other. Traditionally patterned and textured papers available from art stores are also great fun to experiment with.

If you do not live and shop in a major town, you will find Japanese origami paper quite hard to find. You need to look in a good quality arts and craft or specialist paper craft store. You may be able to find a Japanese craft store which should hold a useful stock as well as a selection of books. If you experience problems locating origami paper, write to one of the origami societies listed at the back of this book. They will be able to supply your needs by post and will send you a product and price list plus a few samples if requested.

Origami paper can work out quite expensive. For that reason I practise my folds on lesser quality paper and, when I feel that I have mastered the fold, I will select a better quality sheet of paper that I feel will best reflect the character of the model. Most stationery shops sell jotter blocks of 1000 sheets of either white or coloured paper, size 10 x 10 cm (4 x 4 in). I find these very useful for practise work.

Equipment and Materials

The purist origami exponents frown upon the use of scissors. They say that your end result should be achieved by folding and folding alone. I tend to agree with them in general terms. However, I see nothing wrong with a cut if the result you are seeking cannot be arrived at any other way. Thankfully, the wonderful Japanese folders Isao Honda and Kunihiko Kasahara seem to agree with me and are not adverse to including a necessary cut or two in their work.

Making up the projects described in the Crafty Origami section on pages 24–31 will also need a few additional materials.

Stationery or craft stores will stock your main paper requirements, including tracing paper and card for the templates as well as paper ribbon and card blanks.

PVA medium, a non-toxic adhesive, can be used for most sticking purposes. Where a stronger adhesive is necessary, a hot glue gun is very useful but you only have 15 seconds to make the bond.

Floristry wire, paper wire and floristry tape, needed for the flower and leaf stems and the tendrils on the candelabra, are all available from floristry stores. Stamens for the lilies can be bought at craft stores while coloured sugar is available from sugarcraft stores.

Beads and jewellery findings are all inexpensive and can be found at most craft stores. If you do not own a pair of jewellery pliers, an ordinary pair of long-nosed pliers will do for making the heart necklace and earrings.

Techniques

The folding techniques and origami bases used for the projects in this book are set out in the following pages. Before starting any of the projects, take time to practise these techniques on lesser quality paper.

MAKING A SQUARE FROM AN OBLONG

If you are asked to start with a square piece of paper it is very important that you check that it is absolutely square. You will soon find yourself in trouble if it is not!

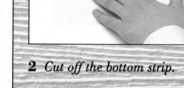

1 Fold the diagonal.

2 Cut off the bottom strip.

3 The complete square.

MAKING AN EQUILATERAL TRIANGLE

All three sides of an equilateral triangle are the same length. This is how you produce one:

1 Start with an oblong piece of paper. Fold it in half along the short side and then open it out again. Valley fold the top left corner over until it touches the centre line that you have just formed. Carefully crease the fold and make sure that the corner is sharp and neat.

2 Fold the right side over, following the line of the top edge of the last fold. Unfold both sides.

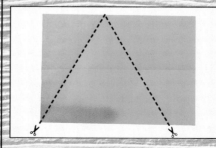

3 You now have two creases. Use scissors or a craft knife to cut along these creases.

4 Your complete equilateral triangle.

THE FOLDING SYMBOLS

In the 1930s a Japanese genius named Akira Yoshizawa devised a system of symbols that he used to describe the folding method of the hundreds of new folds that he was creating. This system has now been universally adopted. It is very easy to learn and quite logical.

1 Valley fold. When opened it looks like a valley.

2 Mountain fold. The opposite to a valley fold.

3 Cut along here. A scissors symbol with a bold dash line.

4 Existing crease. A thin unbroken line.

5 Previous position or X-ray view. A feint dotted line.

6 Hold here. The circle marks the spot where you should hold the model.

7 Watch this spot. The X helps you to keep track of a particular corner when you look at the next illustration. Letters of the alphabet are used when more than one spot has to be kept track of.

8 Fold in front. Usually a valley fold.

9 Fold, then open out again. A doubled-back arrow sign.

10 Fold behind. A white-headed half-arrow.

11 Tuck in. Often used for locking a model.

12 Open out. Open up previously folded parts as directed.

13 Apply force. Press or push in the required direction.

14 Fold over and over. Like a flattened roll.

15 Turn model over. Either from top to bottom or side to side, as directed by the arrow.

16 Rotate. The arrows show you how far.

17 Enlarged view. A larger view is often needed to illustrate minute details of a fold.

18 Accordion pleat. A row of alternating valley and mountain folds.

19 Inflate. Some models have to be blown up. This 'puff arrow' shows you where to blow.

20 Distances are equal. Used for clarity when an uneven number of similar folds are used.

21 Repeat same fold. A similar fold has often to be repeated with similar flaps or corners. The number of cross bars on the arrow tells you how many repeat folds are necessary.

22 Bring together. Two parts must be pulled or joined or sometimes glued together.

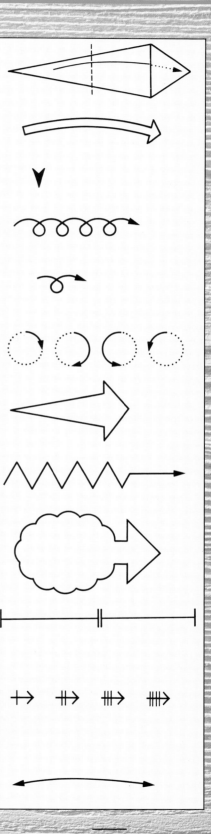

13

FOLDING TECHNIQUES

There are a few basic folding techniques that you should learn. They are all very easy. Grab an odd piece of paper and practise the following:

Inside Reverse Fold

1 Valley fold the paper in half. Hold where shown with your right finger and thumb and push upwards at the 'apply force' symbol with your left thumb.

2 The left half of the paper is turned in on itself and reversed.

3 The creases are sharpened and the inside reverse fold is complete.

Outside Reverse Fold

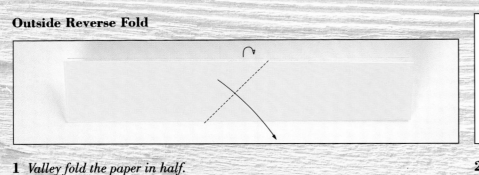

1 Valley fold the paper in half.

2 This time the left half of the paper is turned **out** on itself and reversed.

3 The finished outside reverse fold.

The Crimp
This is used to alter the angle and create a bend in a piece of paper.

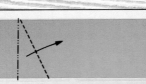

1 Make the mountain and valley folds as illustrated.

2 Push across and flatten the paper into the new position.

The Rabbit's Ear
This is a very commonly used fold.

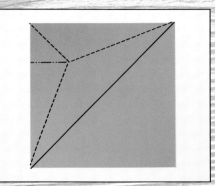

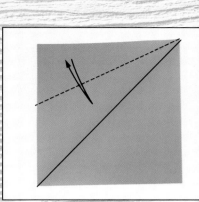

1 *This illustration shows the folds that have to be formed to make a rabbit's ear.*

2 *First valley fold and unfold a diagonal. This is the line that you will work to.*

3 *Now valley fold the top edge to the diagonal centre line and open it out again.*

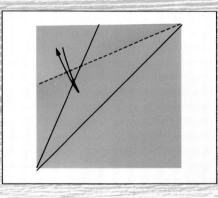

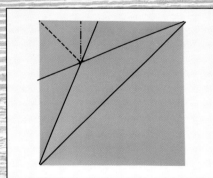

4 *Valley fold the side edge to the diagonal centre line (5) and open it out again.*

6 *Make the small valley fold from the corner to the intersection of the last two valley folds.*

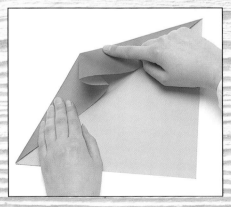

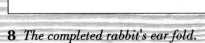

7 *The folds now fall into place.*

8 *The completed rabbit's ear fold.*

THE BASES

There are a handful of bases (basic folds) from which the majority of the models in this book are formed. They are all described in this chapter and can be referred back to as required. All the bases start with a square piece of paper.

The Preliminary Base

The bird and frog bases that follow both start off with the preliminary base.

1 First valley fold the square in half along the diagonal.

2 Then valley fold in half, taking the right side across to the left.

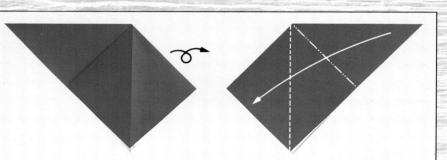

3 Lift up the top layer into an upright position and open up the two thicknesses.

4 Squash fold the top layer into the new position.

5 Turn the model over.

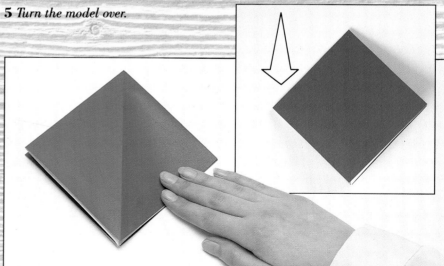

6 Repeat the squash fold on this side.

7 The completed preliminary base.

The Bird Base
Start with the preliminary base.

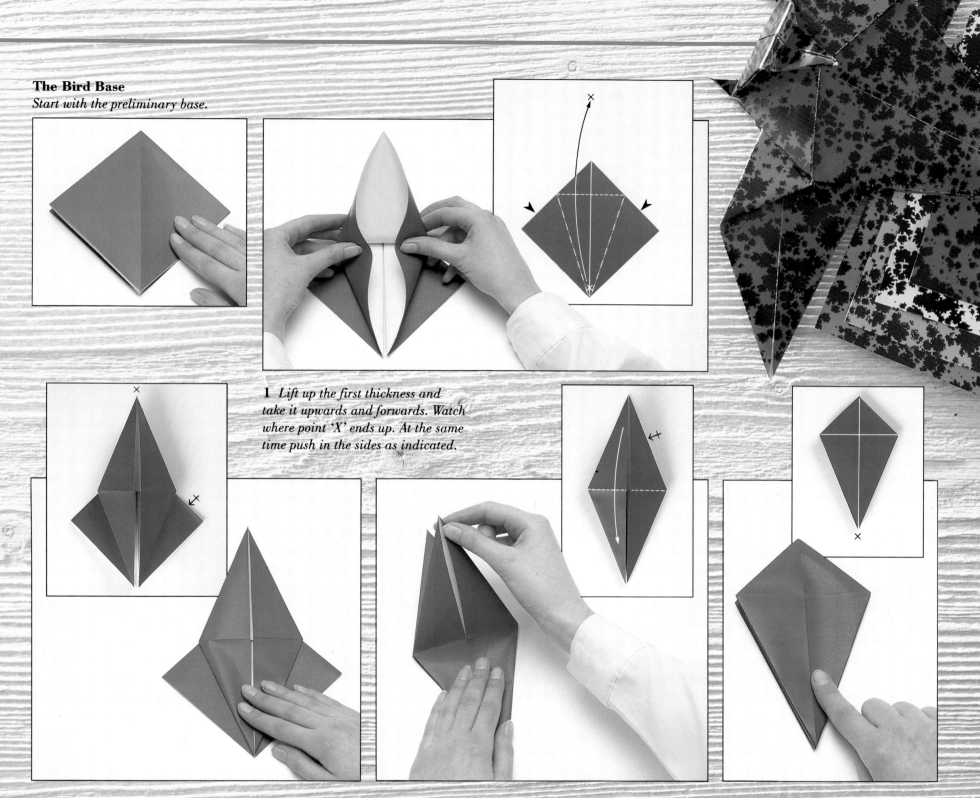

1 *Lift up the first thickness and take it upwards and forwards. Watch where point 'X' ends up. At the same time push in the sides as indicated.*

2 *Press the folds carefully and try to make nice crisp points. Now repeat with the flap at the back.*

3 *Valley fold the flaps downwards, front and back.*

4 *The completed bird base.*

The Frog Base
Start with the preliminary base.

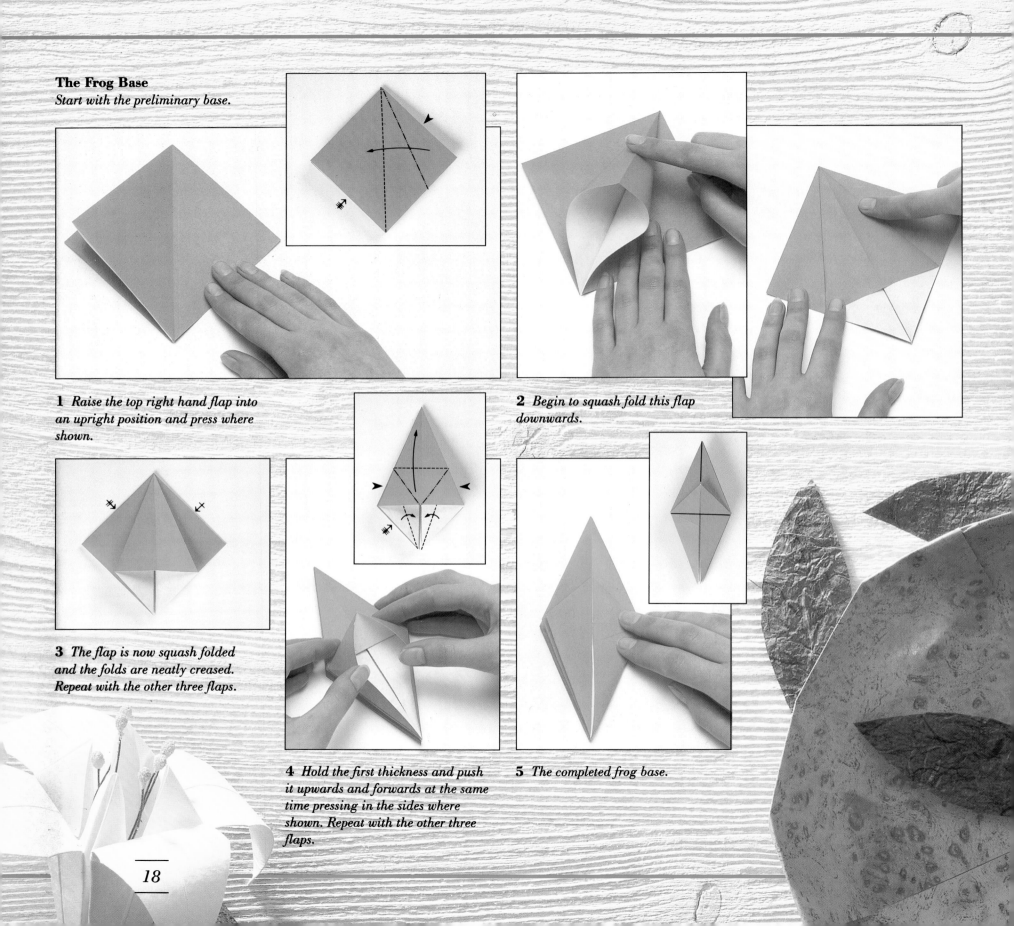

1 *Raise the top right hand flap into an upright position and press where shown.*

2 *Begin to squash fold this flap downwards.*

3 *The flap is now squash folded and the folds are neatly creased. Repeat with the other three flaps.*

4 *Hold the first thickness and push it upwards and forwards at the same time pressing in the sides where shown. Repeat with the other three flaps.*

5 *The completed frog base.*

18

The Blintz Base
This is also a preliminary fold.

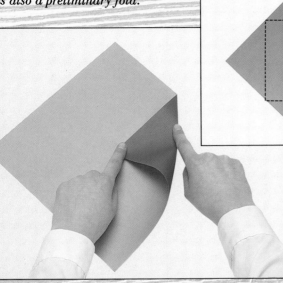 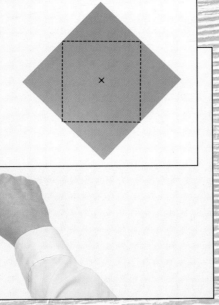

1 *Valley fold the four corners to the centre spot. To locate the centre spot accurately you should first fold the paper in half both ways very lightly.*

2 *The completed blintz base.*

The Diamond Base
First fold a diagonal which you will work to.

The Water Bomb Base
This is a preliminary base turned inside out!

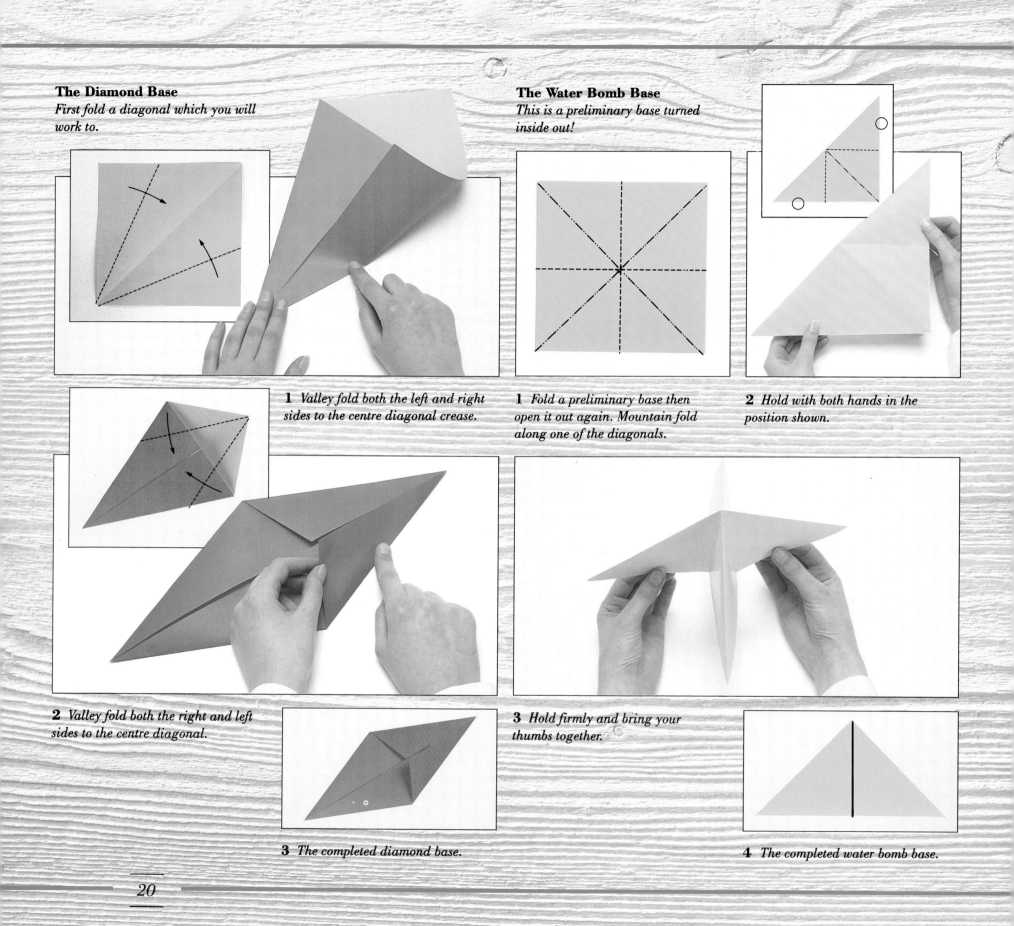

1 Valley fold both the left and right sides to the centre diagonal crease.

1 Fold a preliminary base then open it out again. Mountain fold along one of the diagonals.

2 Hold with both hands in the position shown.

2 Valley fold both the right and left sides to the centre diagonal.

3 The completed diamond base.

3 Hold firmly and bring your thumbs together.

4 The completed water bomb base.

The Fish Base
Start with the diamond base.

1 *Lift out the two hidden corners . . .*

2 *. . . and push them forward.*

3 *Mountain fold to the points and squash fold.*

4 *The completed fish base.*

COMMON FOLDS

The Squash Fold
You will have already done a couple of these but I include this for clarity and completeness. Start with a water bomb base.

1 *Lift the top left flap up into an upright position.*

2 *Open it up and press down on the crease where shown.*

3 *Crease the folds firmly.*

4 *The completed squash fold.*

The Petal Fold 'A'
Carry on from the squash-folded water bomb base that you have just practised.

1 *Lift up the bottom corner and push it upwards and away from you. Press in the sides where shown. Watch corner 'X'.*

2 *This shows the flap on its way.*

3 *The folds are pressed flat to complete the petal fold. Note where point 'X' has ended up.*

The Petal Fold 'B'

Start with a frog base (page 18).

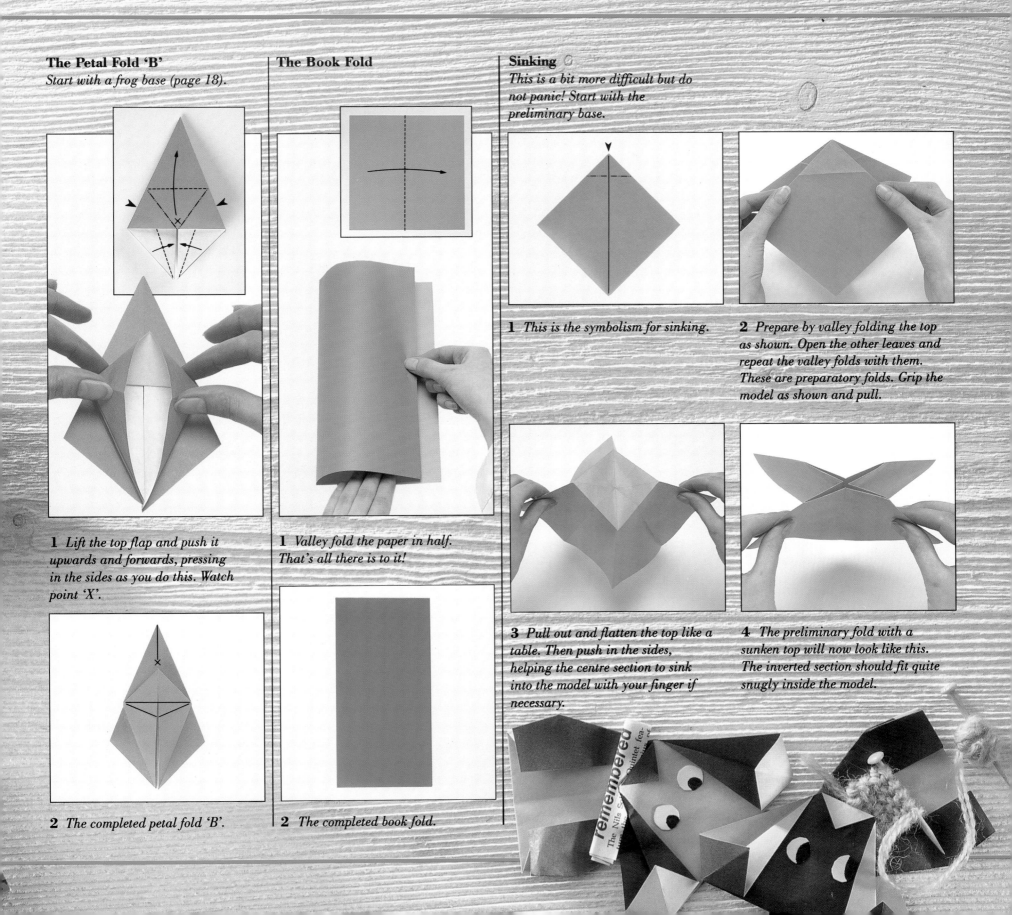

1 Lift the top flap and push it upwards and forwards, pressing in the sides as you do this. Watch point 'X'.

2 The completed petal fold 'B'.

The Book Fold

1 Valley fold the paper in half. That's all there is to it!

2 The completed book fold.

Sinking

This is a bit more difficult but do not panic! Start with the preliminary base.

1 This is the symbolism for sinking.

2 Prepare by valley folding the top as shown. Open the other leaves and repeat the valley folds with them. These are preparatory folds. Grip the model as shown and pull.

3 Pull out and flatten the top like a table. Then push in the sides, helping the centre section to sink into the model with your finger if necessary.

4 The preliminary fold with a sunken top will now look like this. The inverted section should fit quite snugly inside the model.

Crafty Origami

As a form of paper modelling, origami can be cleverly used to make beautiful decorations and gifts. Together with the rich variety of papers available today, the craft techniques described below will transform your origami models into stunning bouquets, wreaths, cards and even jewellery.

LILIES
Page 34

You Will Need:
12 origami lilies (see pages 34–35) made from 23 x 23 cm (9¼ x 9¼ in) square pieces of textured cream paper
1 bunch of long cream stamens
1 bottle of orange coloured sugar (available from sugar craft stores)
Pencil
Piece of card
Tracing paper
1 sheet of dark green giftwrap
PVA glue
Wire cutters
Scissors
1 packet of medium gauge floristry wires
Twelve 30 cm (12 in) lengths of paper wire
1 reel of floristry tape

1 *Mix two tablespoonfuls of PVA glue with one tablespoonful of water in a jam jar. Take 84 of the stamens and dip the head of each one first in the glue and then in the coloured sugar. Leave these to dry and then bundle them into groups of seven, winding the bottoms of the wires around each other to hold them together. Put to one side.*

2 *Trace the template for the lily leaf on page 107 onto a piece of card and cut out. Fold the wrapping paper in two and then using the card template and a pencil draw and cut out 36 pairs of leaves. Cut 18 of the floristry wires into halves with the wire cutters. Taking each pair of leaves, paste one leaf with the glue mixture and lay a wire down the middle so that it does not quite reach one end, but protrudes by a couple of inches at the other end. Lay the other leaf on top of this and wipe over with a damp cloth to remove any surplus glue. Make all 36 leaves in the same way. Allow these to dry, before trimming off any overlap with scissors.*

3 *Take a length of floristry tape and one of the paper wires and, starting at one end, bind the tape diagonally around the wire for approximately 5 cm (2 in). Then, taking one of the wired leaves, lay its protruding wire alongside the paper wire and bind them together with the tape. Add two more leaves in the same way, leaving about 2.5 cm (1 in) between them and placing them on alternate sides of the stem. Continue binding the paper wire to the end. Finish each flower stem in the same way. If the floristry tape is a glaringly different green to the paper, you may wish to paint the stem with a water-based paint, for example, water colours, gouache or poster paint.*

24

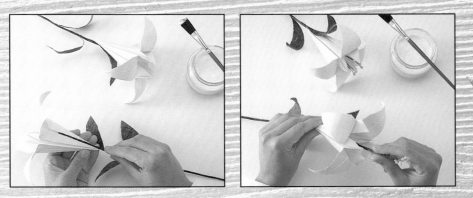

4 *Using undiluted PVA glue, glue the first 5 cm (2 in) of a stem into one of the folds of a lily so that the pointed end of the flower rests just above the first leaf. Put a small dab of glue about one third of the way up this leaf and glue it to the flower to hide the entrance of the wire. Complete the other lilies.*

5 *Put a small blob of undiluted glue onto the base of each group of stamens and push them well down into the centres of the flowers. Arrange the lilies in a vase.*

TULIPS
Page 36

You Will Need:

15 origami tulip flowers (see pages 36–37) made from 21 x 21 cm (8¼ x 8¼ in) square pieces of marbled wrapping paper

3 sheets of Ingres paper in various greens (available in art stores)

Packet of medium-gauge floristry wires

PVA glue

Pencil

Tracing paper

Piece of card

Scissors

Ruler

15 30 cm (12 in) lengths of paper wire

Floristry tape

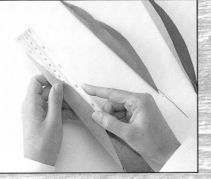

1 *Using the green Ingres paper and the tulip template on page 107, cut out, wire and glue together 30 tulip leaves in the same manner as the lily leaves (see page 24). Use different shades of green on either side of each leaf to get some life-like variations of shade in the flowers. When the leaves are quite dry, trim off any overlap and fold them in half lengthways around the edge of a ruler.*

2 *Take each of the paper wires and remove 4 cm (1½ in) of paper at one end. Curve the bare wires into a loop. Starting at the base of the wire loops, bind the paper wires with floristry tape for about two thirds of the stems' length and then bind in the wires of two matching leaves so that the leaves face each other. Continue binding the stems to the end. Bend the leaves outwards and pinch and twist them a little.*

3 *Dab some undiluted PVA glue onto the wire loop of each stem and carefully insert it into one of the folds of a tulip head so that the stem appears to come out in the correct place at the back of the flower. (If you have a glue gun it will make this slightly tricky manoeuvre a little easier.) Arrange your flowers loosely in a vase.*

CANDELABRA
Page 40

You Will Need:
Approximately 15 simple origami
flowers (see pages 40–41) made
from 7.5 cm (3 in) squares of
marbled gold and green paper
1 metal candelabra
Gold spray paint
Dark green emulsion paint
Medium-sized artist's paint brush
000 gauge (very fine) wire wool
Plastic vine leaves
Forest green paper wire
Low-tack putty
Glue gun and glue sticks
Gold beads

 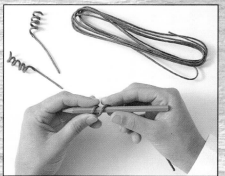 

1 *Spray the candelabra with two or three thin coats of gold paint, allowing each coat to dry thoroughly. Pour three tablespoonfuls of emulsion paint into a jam jar and dilute with water (one part paint to two parts water). Apply a coat of the diluted paint to the candelabra and allow to dry for approximately 30 minutes. Gently rub down the emulsion paint with the wire wool, allowing the gold paint to show through in patches.*

2 *Cut several 10 cm (4 in) lengths of the paper wire and roll them around a pencil to make tendrils. Lay these and several of the smaller vine leaves on a piece of paper and spray randomly with the gold paint. Allow to dry.*

3 *Arrange a design of flowers, tendrils and leaves onto the candelabra, fixing the pieces in place with low-tack putty. When you are satisfied with the effect, remove the low-tack putty and fix the pieces permanently, using the glue gun or some other form of strong glue.*

4 *Finally, glue a small gold bead into the centre of each flower.*

26

WREATH
Page 88

You Will Need:
Two origami cranes (see pages
88–89) made from 25.5 x 25.5 cm
(10 x 10 in) squares of pink,
gold-flecked paper
Approximately 50 small
waterbombs (see pages 88–89)
made from 7.5 x 7.5 cm (3 x 3 in)
squares of purple paper for grapes
1 medium-sized willow wreath
1 tin of gold spray paint
A length of plastic vine leaves
with tendrils
Glue gun and glue sticks
Pink paper ribbon

1 *Lay the willow wreath on a sheet of paper and give it three coats of gold paint, allowing the wreath to dry thoroughly between each coat. Give the vine leaves one random spraying with the gold paint.*

2 *Wind the length of vine around the bottom half of the wreath, fixing both ends with the glue gun and trimming off any leaves that make it look too cluttered. Arrange the leaves and glue in place.*

3 *Build the grapes up into bunches, gluing them onto the wreath and to each other with dabs of glue from the glue gun. Apply the glue to each box on the side with the hole so that the smoothest side is outermost.*

4 *Glue the two cranes onto the wreath in positions that make them appear to be pecking at the grapes. Make a small bow from the paper ribbon. Glue this near the top of the wreath so that it balances the main design.*

WILD GOOSE CARD
Page 90

You Will Need:
1 origami wild goose (see page 90)
made from a 11.5 x 12.5 cm
(4½ x 5 in) square of white paper
15 x 20 cm (6 x 8 in) card blank
Gold poster paint
Old tooth brush or stencil brush
PVA glue
Tracing paper
Small piece of gold card
25 cm (10 in) length of gold ribbon

BUTTERFLY CARD
Page 92

You Will Need:
2 small origami butterflies (see
page 90) made from 7.5 cm (3 in)
squares of paper
15 x 20 cm (6 x 8 in) card blank
1 sheet of floral giftwrap
Small curved nail scissors
PVA glue
Damp cloth
Ruler
Felt pen or coloured pencil

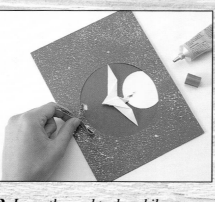

1 *Lay the card out flat with the front uppermost on a piece of paper. Dilute some of the gold poster paint slightly with a little water and stir until it is quite smooth and about the consistency of single cream. Dip your stencil or toothbrush into this mixture and spray by drawing your thumb across the bristles towards yourself. Always spray onto a spare piece of paper first before spraying directly onto the card so that you get rid of any excess paint which will otherwise drip and spoil your design.*

2 *Leave the card to dry while you trace the moon template on page 107 onto the gold card and cut it out. When the gold paint is dry, fold the card back into its normal shape and paste the moon half way down and to the right of the aperture, so that it is partly obscured by the front of the card. Glue on the goose so that his head overlaps the moon and secure the fold-back section to the front with a few dabs of glue. Tie the gold ribbon into a bow and glue onto the side of the card.*

1 *Choose a suitable part of the floral giftwrap design and carefully cut it out with the small scissors. Paste it onto the folded back section of the card so that it shows through the aperture. Put small dabs of glue around the edge of the back of the front of the card so that the folded back section stays in place. Cut out one or two single flowers and leaves and glue them on in such a way that they appear to be part of the main design, but so that they stray across the edges of the aperture. When you have finished, gently wipe off any excess glue with the damp cloth.*

2 *Finally, glue your butterflies on so that they appear to be settling on or flying around the flowers.*

28

PUPPY DOG CARD
Page 92

You Will Need:
1 origami puppy dog (see page 92)
made from two 15 x 15 cm
(6 x 6 in) squares of brown
double-sided origami paper
Small strip cut from a newspaper
Small circles of card for eyes
Felt pen
PVA glue
15 x 20 cm (6 x 8 in) card blank

PUPPY WITH KNITTING
Page 90

You Will Need:
1 origami puppy dog as before
Small amount of fine wool
Fine knitting needles
1 wooden cocktail stick
2 small beads
Strong adhesive
2 small circles of card for the eyes
Felt pen
PVA glue
15 x 20 cm (6 x 8 in) card blank

1 *Draw a black centre to each of the eyes and glue these in place on the face before attaching the whole dog into the aperture on the card. Roll the strip of newspaper into a cylinder and secure it with a dab of glue. Glue the cylinder of newspaper under the mouth.*

1 *Draw two centres to the eyes with the felt pen and glue into position with PVA glue. Cast five stitches onto the knitting needles and knit six rows of plain knitting. Cut the cocktail stick in half and use strong glue to attach a bead onto the blunt end of each. When dry, transfer the knitting onto one of the needles, making sure that the unused wool is at the correct end. Roll the spare wool into a ball and secure with strong glue.*

2 *Glue the dog into the aperture on the card and fix the knitting in its mouth with a dab of strong glue. Glue the little ball of wool onto the front of the card with one of the knitting needles stuck through it.*

29

LOVE-HEART NECKLACE
Page 98

You Will Need:
18 small origami hearts and 1 large
origami heart (see page 98) made
from 5 cm (2 in) and 7.5 cm
(3 in) squares of red
'snake skin' giftwrap
18 small gold beads
Red cotton thread
Needle
1 gold-coloured jump ring
Long-nosed jewellery pliers
50 cm (20 in) of red
leather thonging
Glue gun and glue sticks

1 *Thread your needle with a double
length of red cotton and, starting
with a small heart, thread the
needle through the notch in the top
of the heart and let it come out
through the point. Repeat with a
further eight hearts, threading a
gold bead between each one.*

2 *Place one more gold bead on the
thread before proceeding to thread
the other nine hearts in the reverse
manner, that is, from the point to the
notch. Place a gold bead between
each of these. When you have
completed the final heart, fasten off
the cotton carefully by over-sewing
the top of the back layer of the heart
a couple of times. Tuck the end of
the cotton into the heart.*

3 *Cut the thonging in half and,
using the glue gun, fix one end of
each piece into the tops of the end
hearts. The glue will also serve to
secure the loose end of the cotton.*

DOUBLE-HEART EARRINGS
Page 98

You Will Need:
2 large and 2 small origami hearts
(see page 98) made from 5 cm
(2 in) and 7.5 cm (3 in) green
'snake skin' giftwrap
6 gold-coloured jump rings
1 darning needle
2 gilt-plated flat pad ear studs
2 gilt-plated butterflies
Long-nosed jewellery pliers
1 tube of strong glue

1 *Using the same method as for the
necklace (step 4 this page) fit a jump
ring into the notch of each heart.
Make sure that the jump rings are
closed and then join one large and
one small heart by putting a third
jump ring through the other two and
closing it.*

2 *Put a small amount of strong
glue onto each of the ear studs and,
making sure that your fingers are
nowhere near the glue, hold them in
place on the backs of each of the
smaller hearts for a moment or two.
Make sure that the glue is dry before
sliding on the butterflies.*

4 Using the long-nosed pliers, open the gold jump ring slightly and put to one side. Take the needle and push it through the large heart from front to back and just below the notch. Wriggle it around carefully to make the hole large enough to take the jump ring. Fit the open ring through the hole and then over the cotton between the two gold beads. Close the ring again with the pliers.

SINGLE-HEART EARRINGS
Page 98

You Will Need:
2 small origami hearts (see page 98) made from 5 cm (2 in) squares of red 'snake skin' giftwrap
8 small gold-coloured beads
2 gilt-plated eye pins
2 gilt-plated fish hook ear wires
Long-nosed jewellery pliers

1 Push one of the eye pins, point first, through a heart from point to notch. Thread four beads onto this and then an earwire.

2 Loop the remainder of the wire over with the pliers so that the end disappears back down the hole in the top bead. Finish the other earring in the same way.

TRIPLE-HEART EARRINGS
Page 98

You Will Need:
6 small origami hearts (see page 98) made from 5 cm (2 in) green 'snake skin' giftwrap
4 small black beads
Needle
2 gilt-plated flat pad ear studs
2 gilt-plated butterflies
Strong glue

1 Thread the needle with black cotton and knot the end. Take one of the hearts and push the needle through the notch, pulling the thread out to one side of the point. Push the needle back in on the other side of the point and pull it out again at the notch.

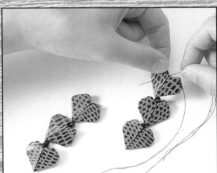

2 Thread one of the black beads onto the cotton and then another heart, point first. Repeat with another bead and heart and then fasten off the cotton by carefully oversewing on the back edge of the heart. Push the needle back into the notch and allow it to come out on one side of the heart. Pull the cotton through and cut off neatly. Finish the other earring before attaching an ear stud and butterfly to the back of both the top hearts as for the double-heart earrings (see step 2, opposite page).

31

Table Talk

Few things look more attractive in your home than a dinner table beautifully laid out with good cutlery, china, wine glasses, napkins beautifully folded and attractive centre pieces. Origami comes into its own here and can be subtly used to stunning effect. Included here are a few interesting projects for you to undertake in the sure knowledge that they will please both you and your guests.

Lilies

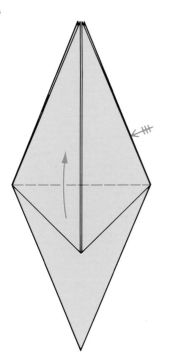

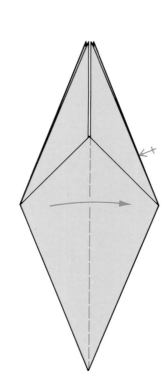

1 *Start with a frog base (see page 18). The open points are at the top. Valley fold all four triangles upwards.*

2 *Book fold a single thickness from the left side across to the right. Repeat behind.*

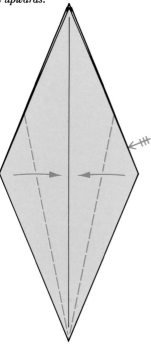

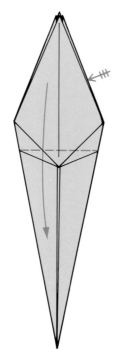

3 *Valley fold the sides to the centre line. Repeat on the other three smooth surfaces.*

4 *Valley fold the four leaves downwards . . .*

◀ *Making flowers out of paper has long been a popular hobby. Origamaniacs have been folding paper flowers for centuries. This beautiful bouquet (see page 24), made out of textured cream paper, is a prime example.*

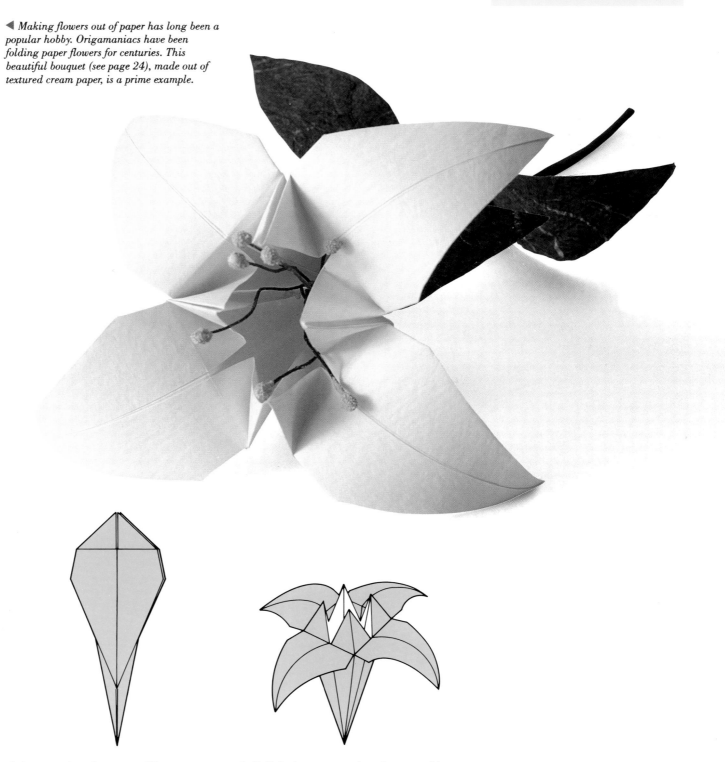

5 . . . *to produce the compact lily.*

6 *Pull the leaves outwards and put a curl in each.*

Tulip and Stem

The Tulip:

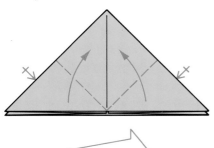

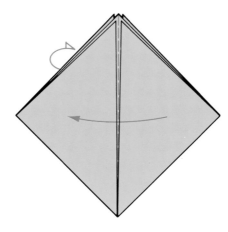

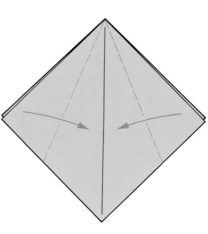

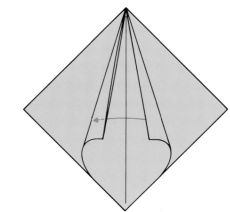

1 *Start with a water bomb base. Valley fold the left and right flaps upwards. Repeat behind.*

2 *Book fold front and back to expose smooth surfaces. This is very important.*

3 *Curl the left and right sides in towards each other.*

4 *Push the tip of the right flap inside the left one. It will not go all the way, but push it as far in as you can.*

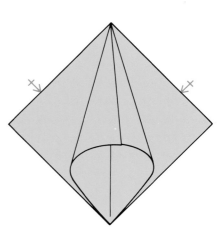

5 *Flatten the linked flaps. Notice that the seam is off centre. Repeat Steps 3–5 behind.*

◀ *Make a bunch of tulips with wire stems (see page 25) and display them in a ceramic vase or in one of the origami vases shown on pages 56–59. Or use different coloured squares for the tulips, choosing green for the stems.*

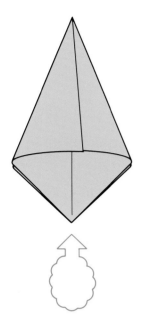

6 *There is a minute hole in the base of the flower. Inflate the model by blowing into this hole. The flower will fill out and the base will flatten.*

The Stem:

7 *The petals will have already loosened slightly. Peel them back carefully and put a curl in the tips.*

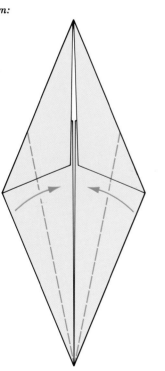

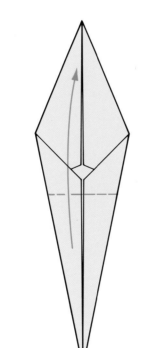

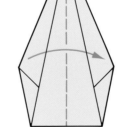

10 *Valley fold the model in half along the centre line.*

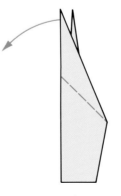

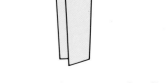

8 *Make a diamond base. Valley fold the left and right sides inwards to the centre line.*

9 *Valley fold the model in half across the centre.*

11 *Outside reverse fold the leaf of the stem and put a slight curl in it.*

12 *Insert the point of the stem into the tulip.*

37

Pagoda

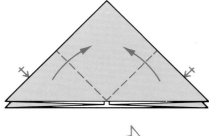

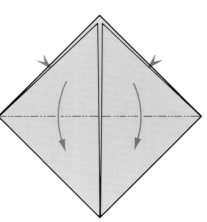

▶ *This impressive model is made from five squares of paper of varying sizes, for instance, 6 cm (2 ½ in), 7 cm (2 ¾ in), 8 cm (3 in), 9 cm (3 ½ in), and 10 cm (4 in). They can either be of the same colour or five different colours, depending upon your personal preference. All five are folded in the same way and nested one on top of the other to form this impressive pagoda.*

1 *Start with a water bomb base (see page 20). Valley fold the lower left and right corners to the centre line. Repeat behind.*

2 *Lift each flap into an upright position. Open them up and squash fold them into square shapes. Repeat behind.*

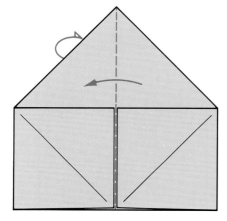

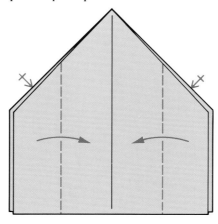

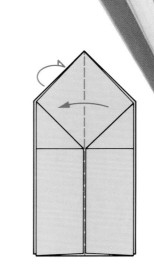

3 *Valley fold the right side to the left. Repeat behind.*

4 *Valley fold the left and right sides inwards to the centre line. Repeat behind.*

5 *Valley fold the right side to the left. Repeat behind.*

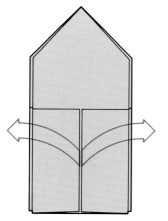

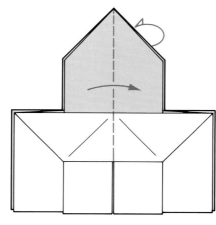

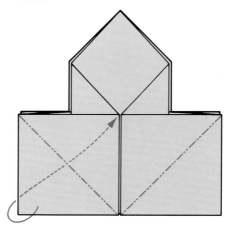

6 *Open up these leaves, pushing them upwards and outwards. Press the mitre corners down flat.*

7 *Valley fold the left side to the right. Repeat behind.*

8 *Mountain fold each bottom square in half and tuck the points up inside.*

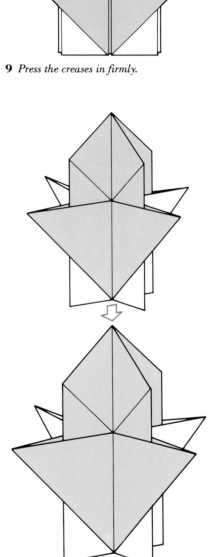

9 *Press the creases in firmly.*

10 *When you have folded all five modules you can assemble them in varying heights to make the magnificent pagoda.*

▲ There are hundreds of simple origami designs. This pretty flower is one of the simplest. Choose your paper carefully to use the flowers as elegant decoration, or make posies out of brightly-coloured floral paper using stamens and wire stems wrapped with floristry tape.

◄ Clusters of blue and gold marbled flowers and an antique finish create a candelabra of sophistication and style (see page 26). The same techniques can be used to create sumptuous candlesticks and table centrepieces.

Simple Flower

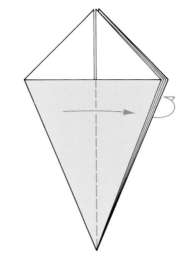

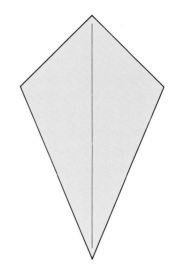

1 Start with step 4 of the frog base (see page 18). Book fold the top flap to the right and the bottom flap to the left . . .

2 . . . revealing smooth surfaces.

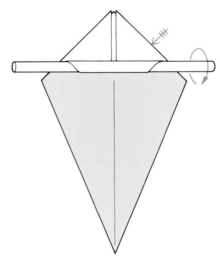

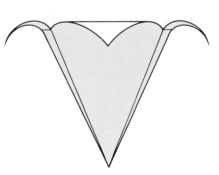

3 Using a tooth pick, knitting needle or other small round object, roll the top triangle around it to form a curl. Repeat with the other three flaps.

4 The flower fold is complete.

Double Swan
You will need two napkins for each person, choosing different colours that complement or contrast with each other.

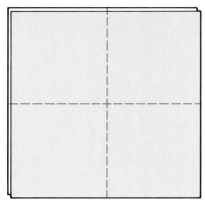

1 *Lay one napkin on top of the other and line them up exactly. Fold them neatly into quarters.*

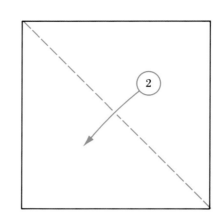

2 *Valley fold two leaves. These will be of different colours.*

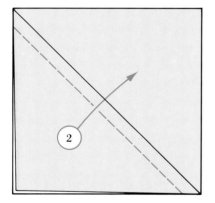

3 *Valley fold both thicknesses back again . . .*

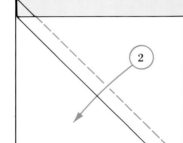

4 *. . . and again . . .*

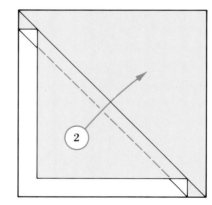

5 *. . . and again . . .*

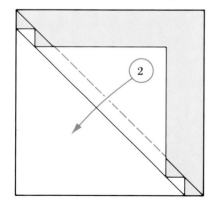

6 *. . . and again. Keep folding in this way until the two thicknesses are completely pleated.*

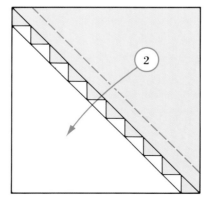

7 *Now fold down the next two thicknesses and pleat them in exactly the same way.*

▶ *This striking fold would grace any dinner table layout. It is very easy to do, yet looks spectacular in contrasting colours of black and white. Experiment with colour combinations to suit your own dining room scheme.*

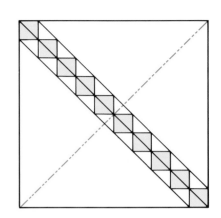

8 *The pleating is complete. Mountain fold the napkins in half across the diagonal.*

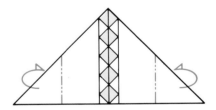

9 *Mountain fold the two sides around and tuck one inside the other. Open out the model and stand it on a plate.*

Fleur-de-Lys
Use crisp, lightly starched napkins for all the napkin folds described in this section.

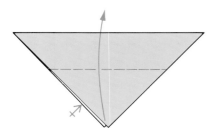

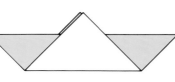

1 *Start by valley folding the napkin across the diagonal to form a triangle.*

2 *Now fold up about two thirds of the front leaf. Repeat behind.*

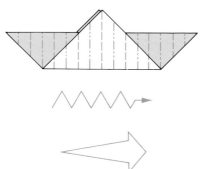

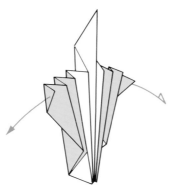

3 *Accordion pleat the entire napkin from left to right, making sure that one of the folds passes directly through the centre point.*

4 *Fan out both sides and . . .*

▶ *The simplest napkin folds are often the most spectacular. Elegantly emulating the ancient heraldic symbol, this fold is perfect for formal dinner parties as a complement to beautiful china and glassware.*

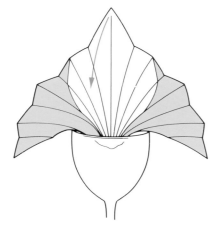

5 *. . . place the napkins into a glass. Fold down the front leaf over the glass. Tease out the sides into a nice fan shape.*

Rabbit

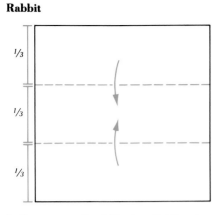

1 *Create two valley folds, thus dividing the napkin into equal thirds.*

2 *Valley fold both sides downwards to the centre line.*

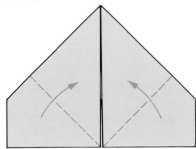

3 *Valley fold both sides upwards to the centre line.*

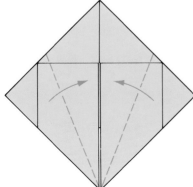

4 *Valley fold both sides upwards to the centre line again.*

▼ *This novelty napkin fold is ideal for children's parties and has long been a favourite at Magic Circle banquets.*

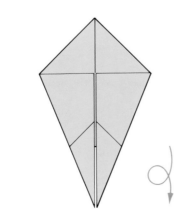

5 *The napkin now looks like this. Turn it over bringing the bottom to the top.*

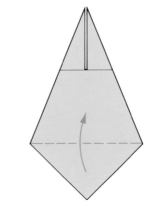

6 *Valley fold the bottom triangle upwards.*

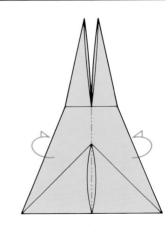

7 *Mountain fold the model along the vertical centre line. Open out the ears and the rabbit is complete. Stand it on a plate.*

Oyster

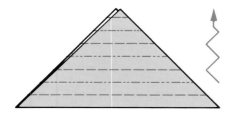

1 *First fold the napkin in half across the diagonal with the points pointing upwards. Now accordion pleat it from bottom to top.*

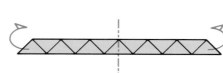

2 *Mountain fold the napkin in half across the centre. This leaves the pleats on the outside. The oyster is complete!*

▶ *This napkin fold takes but a few seconds to do, yet can be used in three different ways. It can simply be laid on the table, where it will naturally fan out. It can be displayed in a wine glass, or one half of it can be tucked under a service plate.*

The Double Flute
You will need two napkins of different and complementary or contrasting colours.

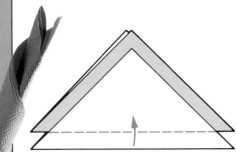

1 *Start by folding both napkins in half across the diagonal. Slide one napkin inside the other but don't align them completely. Valley fold the bottom section upwards.*

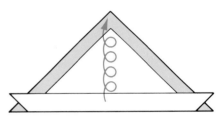

2 *Now roll the napkins upwards and slightly flatten them when you reach the end.*

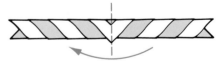

3 *Valley fold the roll in half.*

◀ *Display the double flute in a tall, slim wine glass for the best effect. A display of brightly-coloured paper napkins works well for large buffets or children's parties.*

Container Crazy

Paper folders love making boxes and containers.
Dozens of classic folds are known to origami
folders and new ones are being invented all
the time. This chapter gives examples of both old
and new to hold a range of goodies, from
delicious confectionery to sumptuous
satin ribbons.

Traditional Japanese Box

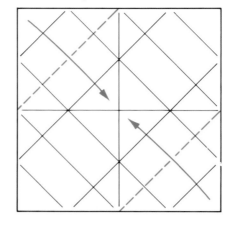 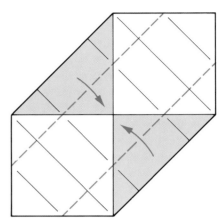

1 *Pre-crease a square of paper with all the diagonal folds indicated. This is quite easily achieved by folding each corner to the centre point and then folding it in half again.*

2 *Fold two opposite corners to the centre point. Pre-crease the four little mountain folds shown. Now valley fold the sides into an upright position.*

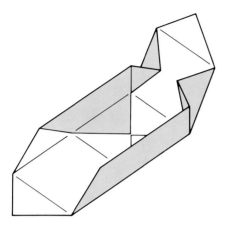

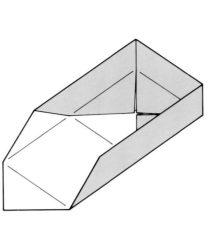

3 *Push in one end and you will find that the mountain and valley folds will fall into place of their own accord.*

4 *Notice how the point of this side lines up with the other two points in the middle. Now push in the other side. Firm up the creases to complete the box.*

◀ *This traditional Japanese fold is probably one of the first box folds ever created. Fold two of these boxes using a slightly larger square of paper to make a lid. If you wish, you can make the sides of the lid slimmer so that it perches on top rather than descends to the bottom of the main box body.*

◀ *Careful choice of the paper used will produce boxes for every occasion. Use Christmas giftwrap for seasonal giftboxes, seek out jewel-coloured patterned papers to contain your favourite trinkets, and make use of subtle marbled papers for boxes to keep small desk items tidy.*

51

Star Box

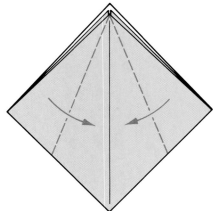

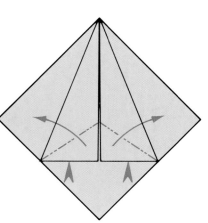

1 *Start with a preliminary base (see page 16) with the points facing upwards. Valley fold the top layers as shown.*

2 *Lift each flap into an upright position. Open each one up and squash fold them both, following the mountain folds and pressure points.*

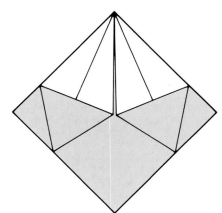

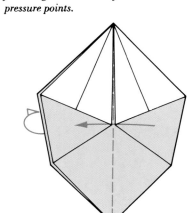

3 *Repeat behind.*

4 *Book fold the right side to the left. Repeat behind.*

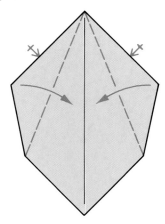

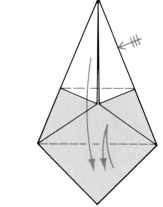

5 *Valley fold the sides to the centre line.*

6 *Valley fold the top flap downwards.*

◀ *This lovely container is valued by origami folders as much for its decorative qualities as for its usefulness.*

7 *Repeat with the other three points.*

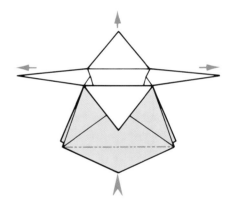

8 *Gently pull the four points outwards and press the bottom inwards. Now put your fingers inside the box and fix its form by pressing all the creases in firmly.*

Gift Box

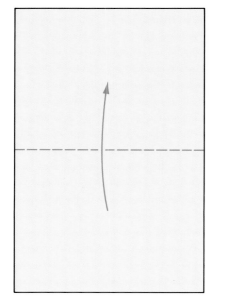

1 *Use a fairly stiff sheet of paper with 3 x 2 proportions. Valley fold upwards in half.*

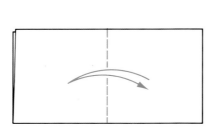

2 *Book fold in half and open up again.*

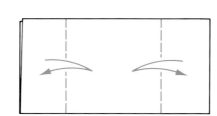

3 *Valley fold the left and right sides to the centre line. Open up again.*

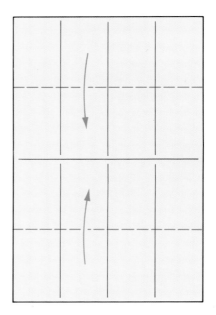

4 *Open the sheet completely. Valley fold the top and bottom edges to the horizontal centre line.*

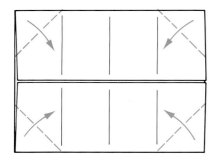

5 *Valley fold the four corners. Note that these only reach to the quarter line and not the horizontal centre line.*

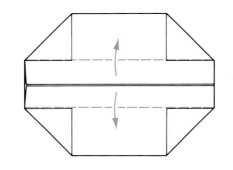

6 *Fold up the two centre edges over the folded corners.*

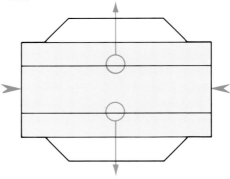

7 *Hold where shown and pull gently outwards, at the same time pushing in the sides where shown by the pressure symbols.*

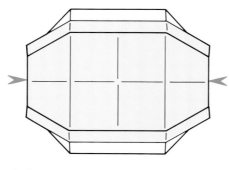

8 *Keep pulling and pushing and firm up the box edges that have now formed.*

▶ *Folders love making boxes. The gift box is among the first known examples of the hundreds of different models that have been produced over centuries of folding.*

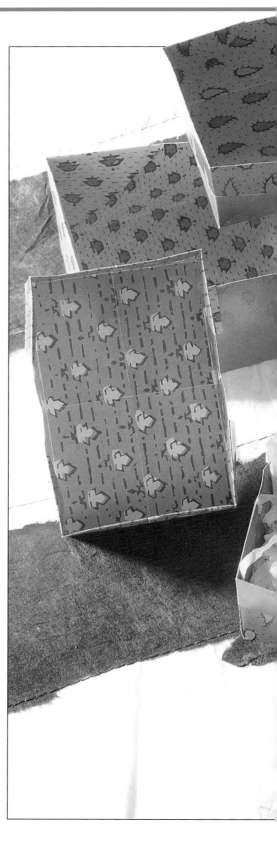

Container Crazy

Traditional Chinese Vase
This is a difficult fold. Take your time with it. Start with any old square of paper and, once you have mastered the fold, choose the most beautiful square of paper that you can find.

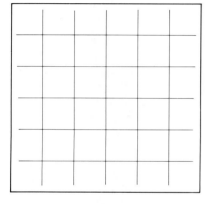

1 *Use a double-sided large square of paper. The paper has to be divided into 36 equal squares (6 x 6). Eventually you will be able to judge this with your eye but, to begin with, use a ruler to divide the paper up accurately. Pre-creasing the paper in halves both vertically and horizontally will start you off.*

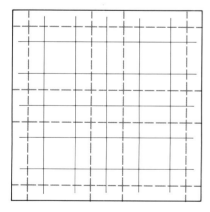

2 *Valley fold in the eight places indicated with great care. Open up all the folds again.*

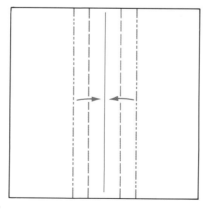

3 *Mountain and valley fold each side to the centre line. Crease firmly.*

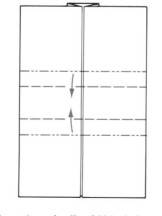

4 *Mountain and valley fold both the top and bottom to the centre line.*

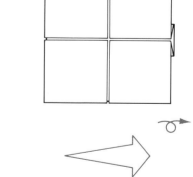

5 *Turn the model over.*

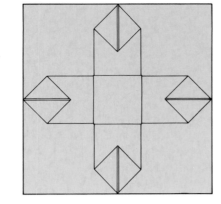

7 Turn the model over.

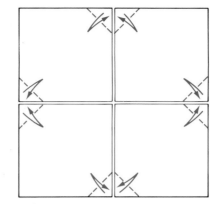

8 Look at the eight corners indicated. Valley fold then unfold each one. This is important preparation for later.

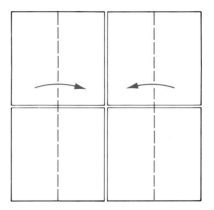

9 Valley fold both sides inwards.

10 Valley fold the top and bottom . . .

11 . . . and tuck the corners away. Mountain fold the four tips out of sight to form the lips of the vase. Turn the model over.

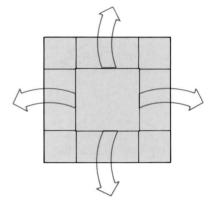

12 Gently pull out the four straps, releasing the folds that you previously trapped in steps 3, 4 and 5. At the same time, put your fingers inside the vase and mould out the shape.

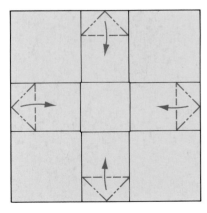

6 Open out each of the four sections and squash fold them flat, following the mountain and valley folds.

◄ You will get such a thrill if you persevere with this model. The final expansion and shaping out is quite wondrous. It is a traditional Chinese design and anyone attempting it is, once more, left to wonder at the ingenuity of its creator.

Rectangular Vase

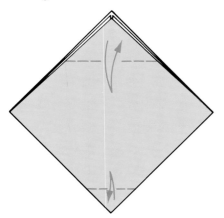

1 *Use a square piece and start with a preliminary base (see page 16) with the open points facing upwards. Fold the top layer down to the centre point and open up again. Fold and unfold the bottom upwards. This is one eighth of the model.*

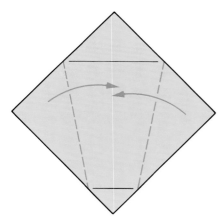

2 *Valley fold the left and right sides inwards. The two previous creases indicate the correct angle.*

▶ *If you choose your paper carefully, this fold will be found to be most effective. Its angular shape makes it especially suitable for emulating Japanese and Chinese style pottery.*

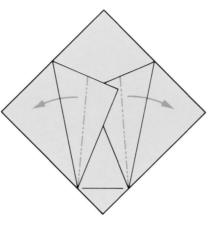

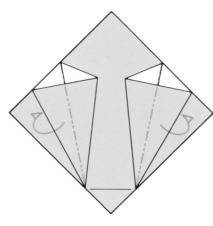

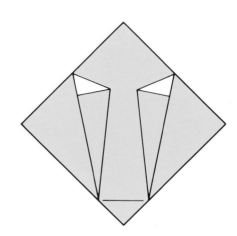

3 *Lift up each flap and squash fold them.*

4 *Mountain fold the sides of these flaps behind . . .*

5 *. . . like this. Now turn the model over and repeat steps 1–4 on this side.*

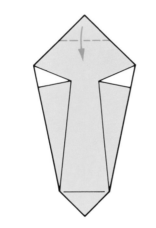

6 *Valley fold the top flap down once . . .*

7 *. . . twice . . .*

8 *. . . and a third time.*

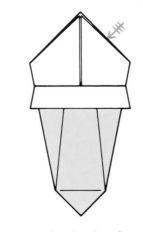

9 *Repeat with the other three flaps.*

10 *Open out the vase and flatten the base following your earlier guide lines.*

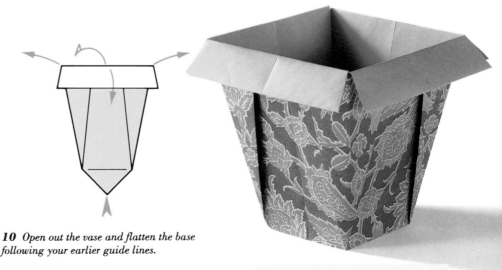

Bowl by Aldo Putignano

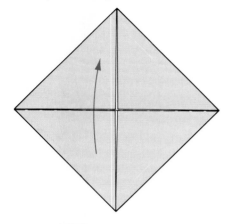

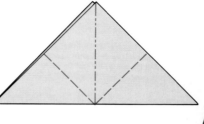

1 *Start with a blintz base (see page 19). Valley fold the model in half across the horizontal diagonal.*

2 *Follow the valley and mountain folds shown to form the triangular shape into a water bomb base.*

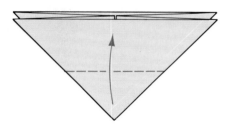

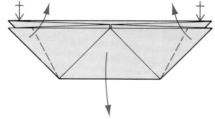

3 *Valley fold the bottom point to the top.*

4 *Valley fold the left and right sides as shown (note the angle). Repeat with the two rear flaps. Unfold the pointed triangle.*

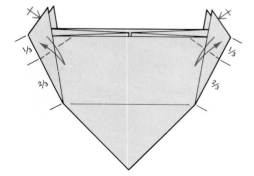

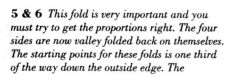

5 & 6 *This fold is very important and you must try to get the proportions right. The four sides are now valley folded back on themselves. The starting points for these folds is one third of the way down the outside edge. The*

drawing will make this clearer. Step 6 shows the folds completed. Now these guideline folds have been put in place the four points should be unfolded again so that the model once more represents step 5.

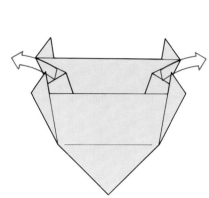

7 *Carefully open out the model.*

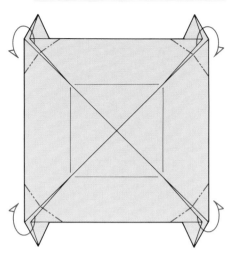

8 *This shows an inside view of the bowl. Mountain fold the four corners following the guidelines marked.*

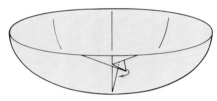

9 *Mountain fold all four little pointed flaps and tuck them into the little pockets. Shape out the bowl with your fingers.*

◀ *This fold is quite extraordinary as the original task set was to fold a bowl from a square piece of paper. This has been brilliantly achieved by Aldo Putignano and its simplicity is an object lesson for all origami students.*

Traditional Baker's Basket

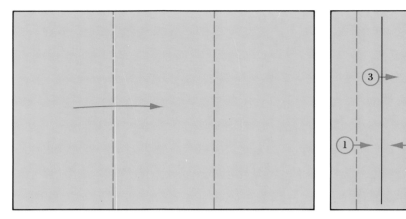

1 *As both sides of the paper appear in the finished model, it is best to use double-sided paper or even stick two pieces of paper back to back. Your starting size should be of 2 x 1 proportions, for example, 40 x 20 cm (16 x 8 in). Fold the paper into four along its length* and then cut off one quarter. You will use this *piece eventually to make the basket handle. Taking the remaining 30 x 20 cm (11¾ x 8 in) piece, valley fold the left third to the right following your previous fold.*

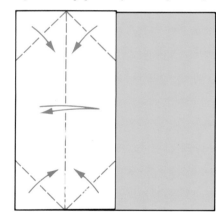

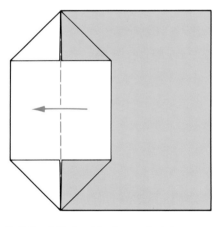

2 *Valley fold the right side of this flap to the left and then open it out again. Now valley fold the four corners to meet this crease.*

3 *Valley fold the right flap to the left.*

▶ *This is a traditional baker's basket fold that originated in Europe and is still used in some countries to package small cakes and biscuits. You can use it to present gifts, from confectionery to jewellery.*

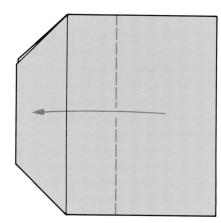

4 *Valley fold the right third to the left following your initial crease.*

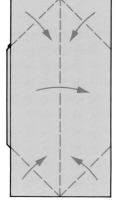

5 *Make a vertical centre crease line in this section and then fold in the four corners as shown. Finally fold the left side to the right.*

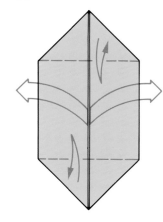

6 *Fold and unfold the top and bottom triangles. Now open up the tray section and shape it out . . .*

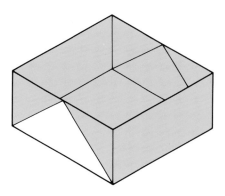

7 *. . . until it looks like this.*

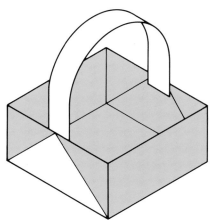

8 *Make the basket handle by giving the strip three folds and fixing the final fold with glue or double-sided sticky tape so that it does not unroll. Glue or staple the handle to the tray and your baker's basket is complete.*

Carrier Bag

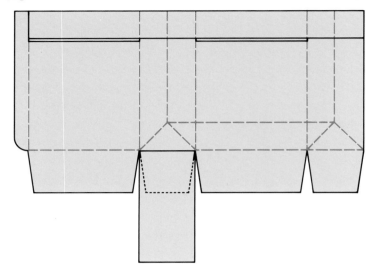

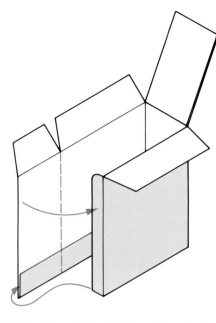

1 *Trace the template on page 107 onto fairly stiff paper of 5 x 3 proportions. Cut out and score along all the dotted lines.*

2 *Turn the model upside down. Crease in the folds to form the box shape and glue the last flap onto and over the little end flap. The lower edge of the little flap slides inside the edge of the very long flap that you folded initially. This creates greater stability.*

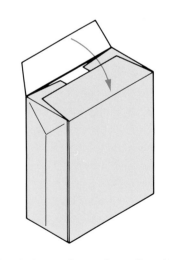

3 *Glue the bottom flaps to the cardboard base section in the order shown.*

▶ *You will need relatively strong papers to make these glorious carrier bags. Thin cord is available in a variety of colours to complement or contrast with the giftwrap. In place of cord, ribbon or even string can be used.*

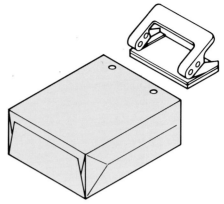

4 *Use an office paper punch to form holes centrally along both top edges.*

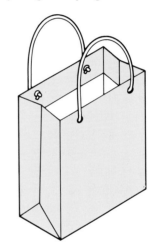

5 *Thread the cords through the holes and knot the ends. The carrier bag is complete.*

6 *The carrier bag will fold flat in a very neat way if you follow the edge folds that you scored originally.*

Clever Creatures

Probably every animal known to man has had the 'origami treatment' at some time or other. Included in this chapter is a selection of birds and animals that will increase your pleasure in origami as well as enhancing your confidence, and even your reputation, as a folder.

Flamingo by Jon Tremaine

▶ *The beauty of the flamingo's plumage is even more spectacular when these elegant birds are seen en masse. As an origami fold, the flamingo creates some interesting problems.*

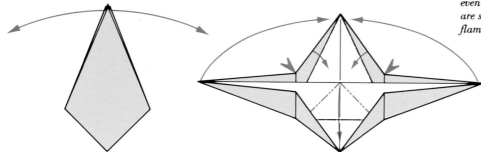

1 *Start with a bird base (see page 17). Pull the two inside flaps outwards as far as they will go.*

2 *Bring the two points together at the top and at the same time push the centre pointed section downwards following the mountain folds. Fold the model flat. This is called a stretched bird base.*

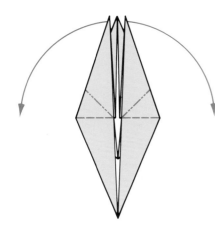

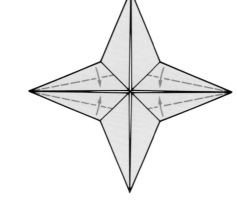

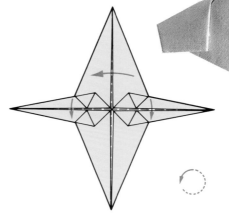

3 *Lift the left flap upright. Open it up and squash fold it outwards. Repeat the squash fold with the right flap.*

4 *Valley fold the top and bottom sides of each flap inwards to the centre line.*

5 *Fold the flaps in half downwards. Now book fold the entire model in half. Rotate the model 90 degrees.*

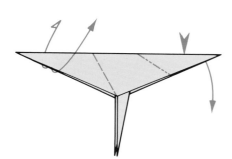

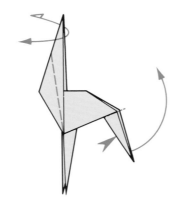

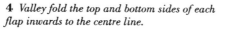

6 *Inside reverse fold the tail downwards. Outside reverse fold the chest and head section upwards.*

7 *Outside reverse fold the chest and head section back again. Make sure that you get the angle right. Inside reverse fold the tail again.*

8 *Make one more outside reverse fold to the neck and chest section. Tuck the tip of the tail inside and then fold the tail section over the body, following the mountain and valley fold indicators.*

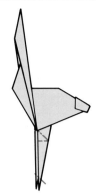

9 *Shape the nearest leg with three inside reverse folds as shown. The rear foot is formed with one small outside reverse fold.*

10 *Outside reverse fold the head and inside reverse fold the beak.*

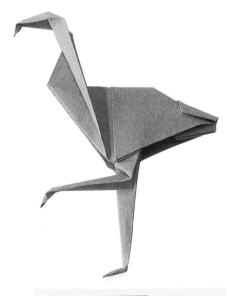

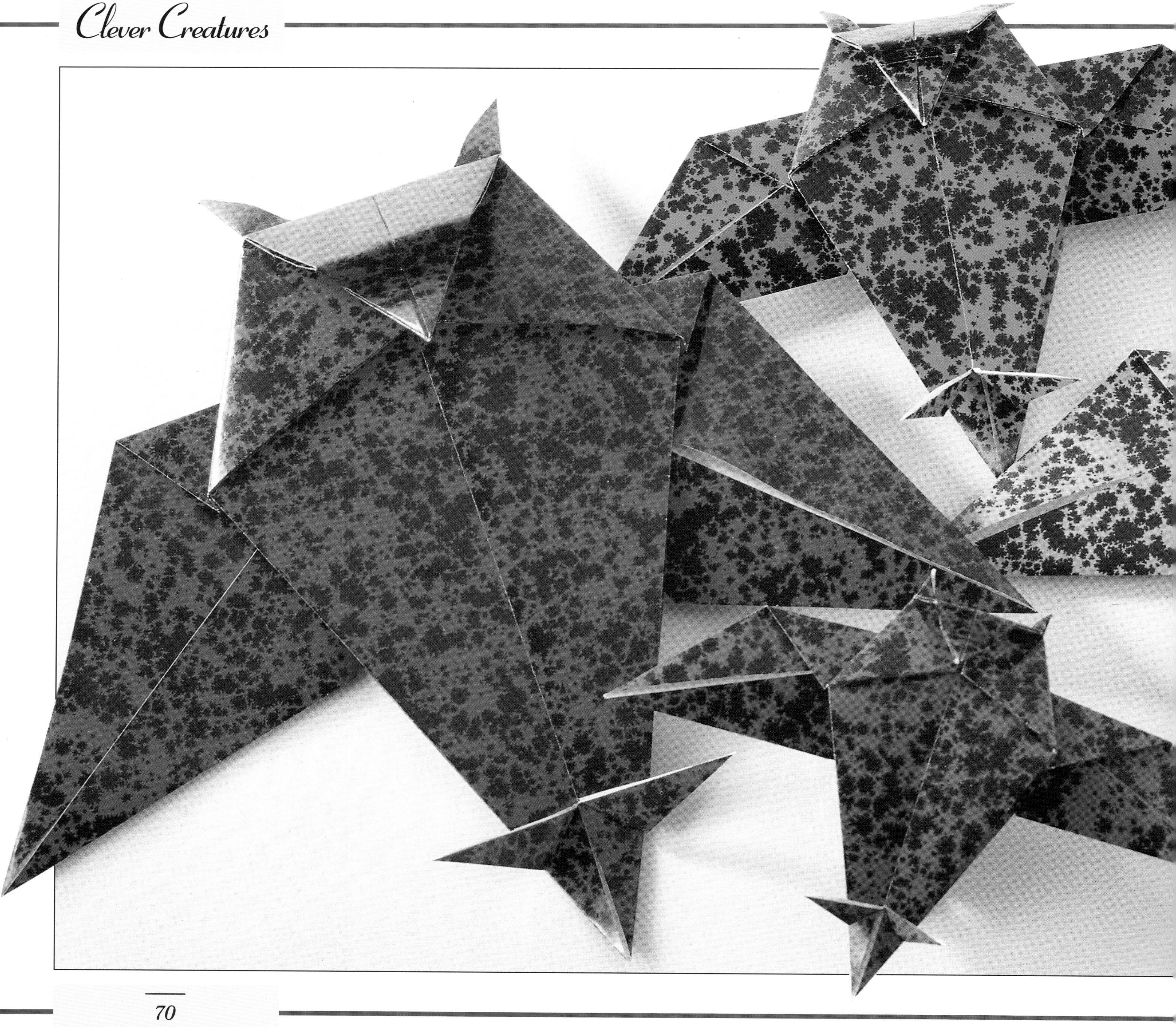

Owl

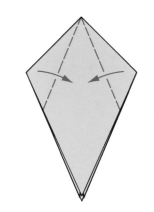

1 *Start with a square piece of paper and fold it into a bird base (see page 17). With all the points pointing downwards, valley fold the top left and right layers to the centre line.*

2 *Mountain fold the lower two flaps behind.*

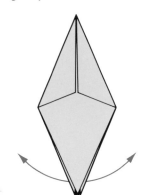

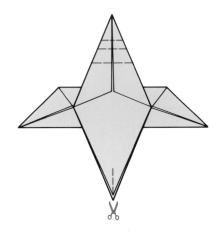

3 *This is a bit tricky! Pull out the inner two points and . . .*

4 *. . . re-press the creases firmly to form the wings. This is almost like an inside reverse fold. Make a little cut in the top lower leaf only. This is to facilitate the foot fold. Make the three head folds in sequence. First a mountain fold behind, then the two valley folds.*

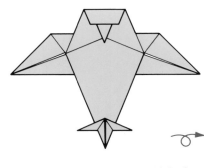

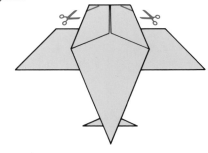

5 *This shows the formed head. Fold the feet to left and right.*

6 *Turn the model over. Make the two ear incisions and then push the ears upwards.*

Peacock
Use two square pieces of paper of the same size. Fold the first piece into a bird base (see page 17) then work through the following steps:

The Body:

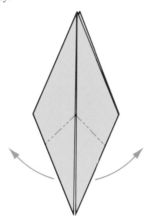

1 *Inside reverse fold both bottom points as far as shown.*

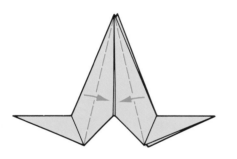

2 *Valley fold the top left and right sides inwards towards the centre.*

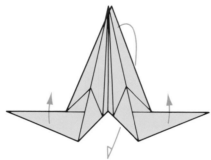

3 *Drop the back flap right the way down to the bottom behind. Open up both leg sections.*

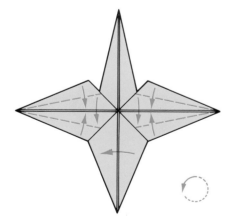

4 *Narrow the legs by valley folding the sides inwards. Then fold each one in half. Valley fold the complete model in half down the centre line. Rotate the model 90 degrees.*

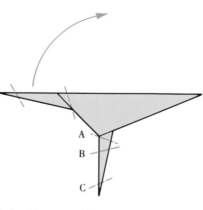

5 *Outside reverse fold the neck at the shoulder, then outside reverse fold the head back again. The legs are folded like this:*
(a) inside reverse fold the legs backwards,
(b) inside reverse fold the legs forwards,
(c) outside reverse fold the feet.

The Fan and Tail:

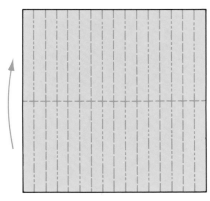

6 *Accordion fold the second square of paper with alternate valley and mountain folds. Press the creases firmly. When you have done that, valley fold the pleats in half.*

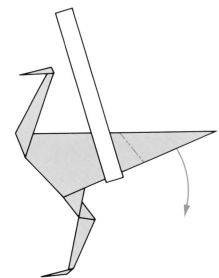

7 *Place the fan in position on the peacock's body and secure with a little glue or double-sided sticky tape. Glue the two centre parts of the tail fan together so that they hold their fan shape. Reverse fold the tail downwards so that it acts as a prop for the body.*

◀ *Try to find paper with a marbled pattern for this model. Displayed as an ornament, the peacock will arouse great interest.*

73

Elephant

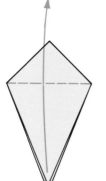

1 *Start with a bird base (see page 17). Valley fold the top flap upwards.*

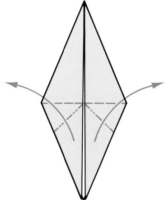

2 *Lift the two flaps upwards and squash fold them to the left and right.*

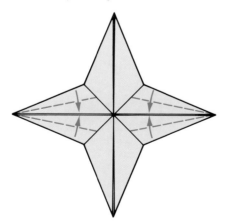

3 *Valley fold both sides inwards to narrow the points.*

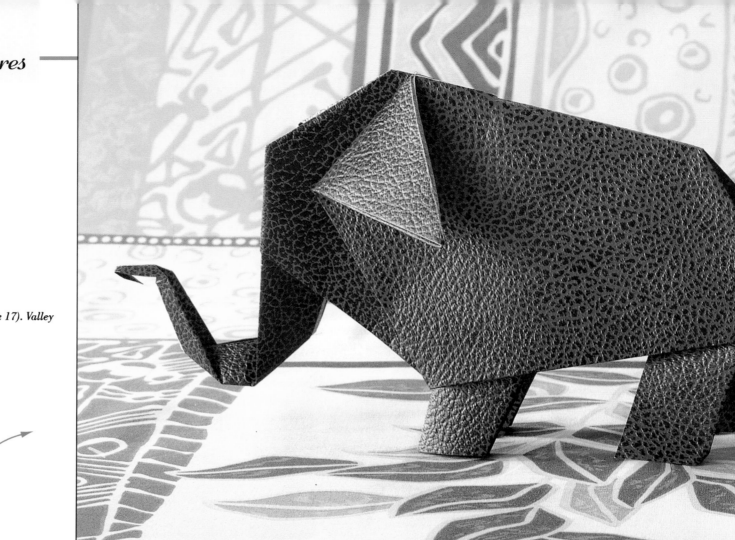

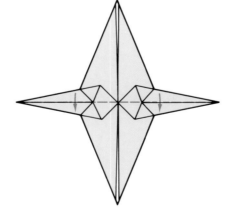

4 *Valley fold the tops downwards to narrow these points further.*

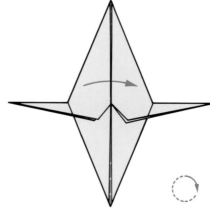
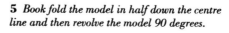

5 *Book fold the model in half down the centre line and then revolve the model 90 degrees.*

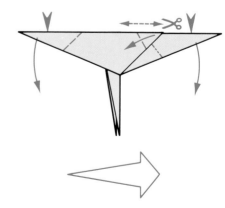

6 *Inside reverse fold the rear. Cut along the top section as shown to form the ears. Valley fold them back. Inside reverse fold the head section to form the trunk.*

◀ *The enormous variety of papers available today is demonstrated by these models, made of paper that mimics the texture of elephant hide – and at the same time adding a splash of colour! These elephants were made in varying sizes and joined trunk to tail to form their traditional procession.*

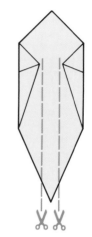

11 *To form the tail, open up the back and make two careful cuts as shown. This will separate the legs and also give you a tail. Give the tail a couple of twists.*

7 *Narrow the back legs with mountain folds. Narrow the trunk by two mountain folds as shown.*

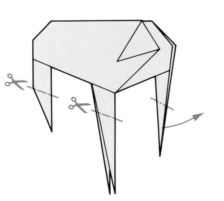

8 *Trim off the legs to make them short and stubby. Inside reverse fold the trunk.*

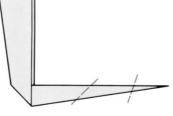

9 *Finish the trunk off with an outside and then an inside reverse fold.*

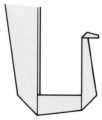

10 *The folded elephant trunk should look like this.*

Three Wise Monkeys by Jon Tremaine

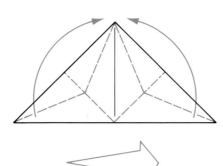

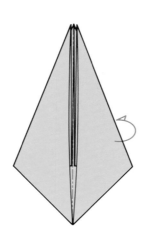

1 *You need a triangle of paper (cut a square across the diagonal) for this model. Rabbit ear fold the left and right sides upwards alongside the centre line.*

2 *Mountain fold the model in half.*

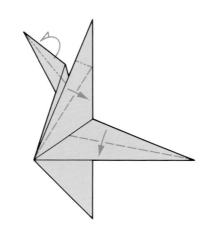

3 *Valley fold the top flap down out to the right side and the bottom flap outwards and upwards to the left.*

4 *Narrow both arms with folds as shown. Open up the chest and head section to the right as far as it will go . . .*

▶ *By varying the position of the arms and hands on these models, these monkeys delightfully illustrate the old maxim 'hear no evil, see no evil, speak no evil'.*

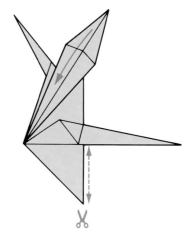

5 . . . and fold the head down pressing in the creases firmly. Cut the bottom section as shown to form two legs.

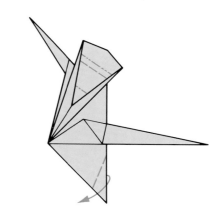

6 Mountain and valley fold the head as shown. Outside reverse fold both legs to form feet. Fold the arms and hands of each monkey as illustrated.

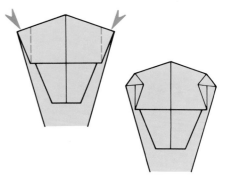

7 & 8 Squash fold the ears.

Persian Cat by Jon Tremaine
Use two squares the same colour and size for this model.

The Head:

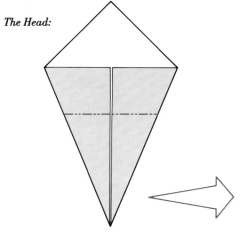 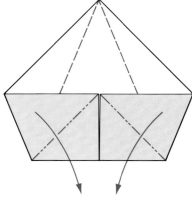 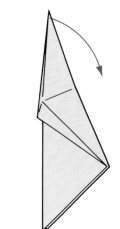 

1 *Start by folding the first square as far as step 2 of the diamond base (see page 20). Mountain fold in half bringing the two points together behind.*

2 *Petal fold as shown.*

3 *Book fold the model from left to right.*

4 *Open up and form the head with a squash fold . . .*

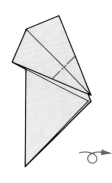

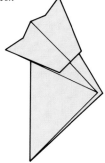

5 *. . . as shown*

6 *Mountain fold the tip of the nose under. Turn the model over.*

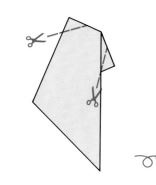

7 *Make two 'ear snips' as shown, being careful to cut only through the top surface. Turn the model over.*

8 *This shows the completed chest and head section.*

The Body:

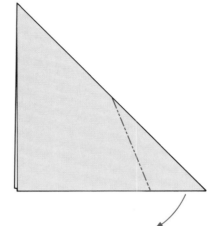

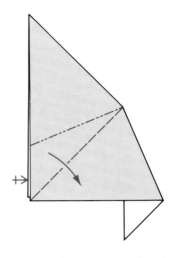

9 *Fold the second piece of paper in half across the diagonal. Inside reverse fold the point as shown.*

10 *Crimp the left side as shown, bringing the top half of the diagonal side into a horizontal position.*

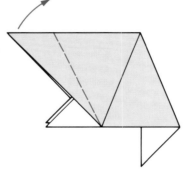

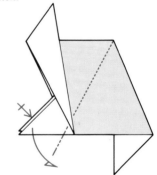

11 *Outside reverse fold the tail.*

12 *Mountain fold the back legs.*

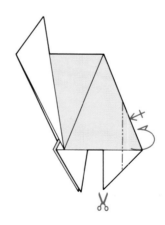

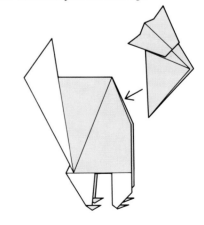

13 *Separate the front section with a scissor cut to form two front legs. Put mountain folds in them to make them narrower.*

14 *Stick the two halves of the Persian cat together. Outward reverse fold the back feet and mountain fold the front feet.*

Festive Flair

Paper has long been used for festive and decorative purposes both in Japan and the western world. The stunning selection of decorative folds contained in this section will enhance your gifts and grace your festivities wherever you happen to be celebrating.

Oriana Star by Jon Tremaine

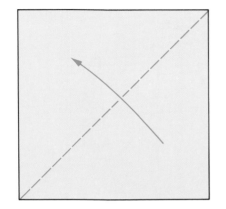

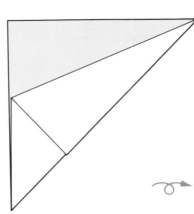

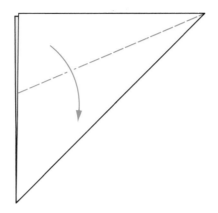

1 *You will need eight squares to make the Oriana star. Treat each square in the same way. Valley fold in half across the diagonal.*

2 *Valley fold the top leaf back to the diagonal edge.*

3 *Turn the model over.*

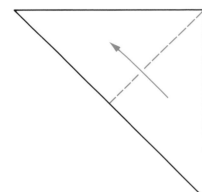

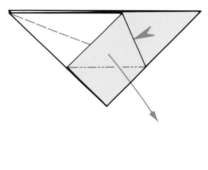

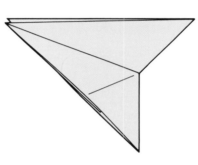

4 *Valley fold in half.*

5 *Squash fold following the valley and mountain folds.*

6 *The finished fold. Now fold the remaining seven squares in the same way.*

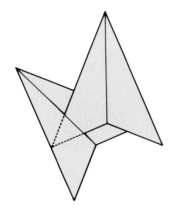

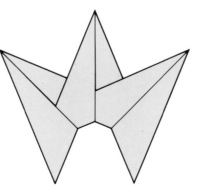

7 *Insert the point of one module into the secret pocket of another.*

8 *Insert the next one in the same way.*

9 *All eight sections are now linked together. The eighth module is now tucked under the first one and the point of the first module is inserted into the secret pocket of the eighth.*

▲ *The original Oriana Star was invented to celebrate the launch of a new super liner. May it bring good fortune to the ship as well as festive delight to those celebrating on dry land.*

Pomander

Both sides of the paper are shown in the finished model so choose a contrasting double-sided paper. If your paper is coloured on one side and white on the other, you should start with the coloured side downwards.

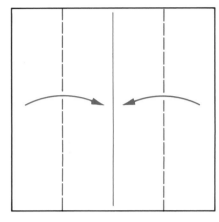

1 *Valley fold both the left and right sides inwards to the centre line.*

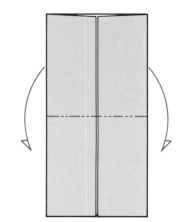

2 *Mountain fold in half.*

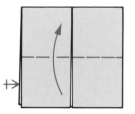

3 *Valley fold upwards. Repeat behind.*

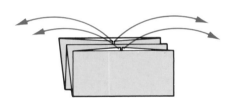

4 *The four loose points are now pulled out . . .*

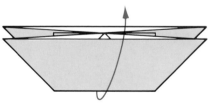

5 *. . . and refolded into pointed hulls. Now open up the model flat.*

6 *Lift up each of the four corners in turn and squash fold them into squares, applying pressure where shown.*

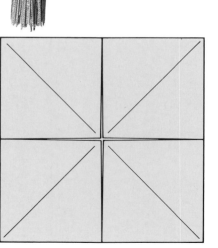

7 *Your model now looks like this.*

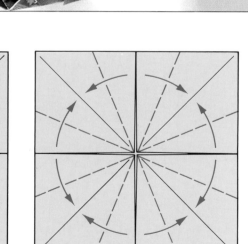

8 *Valley fold the eight flaps inwards towards the diagonal centre lines . . .*

◀ *The coaster module that makes up the pomander is also very useful as a drinks coaster or as decorative addition to an origami box. Choose your paper carefully and you will be rewarded by stunning results.*

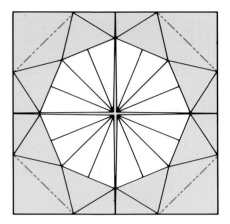

12 *All eight are now folded. Mountain fold the four corners behind.*

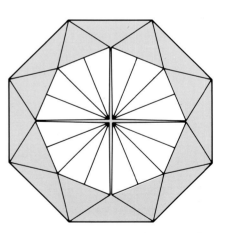

13 *The finished module before being made into the pomander. Make six of these modules altogether. Lift up the folded down corners and, referring to the diagram on page 106, stick the triangular tabs of the six modules together in the shape of a cross. Then stick the remaining tabs together A to A, B to B, etc., until the pomander shape is completed. The completed pomander can be suspended by thread from the ceiling or hung on your tree.*

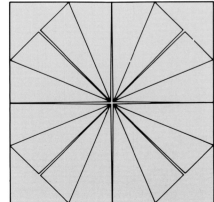

9 *. . . like this.*

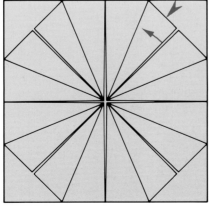

10 *Lift each of the eight little flaps into an upright position and squash fold them . . .*

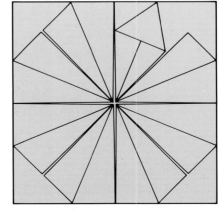

11 *. . . like this.*

Princess
Choose a beautiful square of paper and start with the coloured side down.

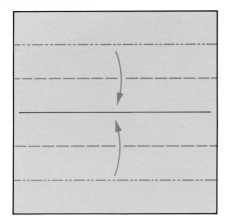

1 *Valley and mountain fold each half of the paper into the centre line, dividing each half into equal thirds.*

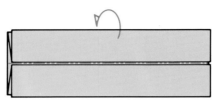

2 *Mountain fold in half.*

3 *Valley and mountain fold each side to the centre line as before.*

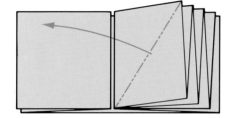

4 *Starting on the right side, open up each of the three leaves . . .*

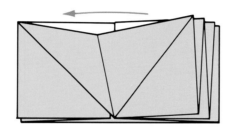

5 *. . . and squash fold them . . .*

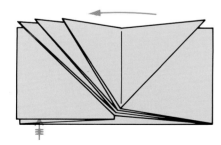

6 *. . . into triangles. Repeat with the three points on the other side.*

▶ *Metallic Christmas giftwrap, whether patterned or plain, is perfect for creating these extravagant decorations. Choose a paper that is coloured on one side only for the princess and a double-sided paper for the palm leaf.*

◀ *Two of the most beautiful napkin folds have been adapted here to make stunning giftwrap decorations. Used as place settings, the princess can be laid on a plate with a flower between the centre folds, while the palm leaf looks stunning displayed in a wine glass.*

Palm Leaf

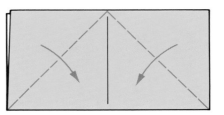

1 *Valley fold the paper in half, positioning the open ends at the top.*

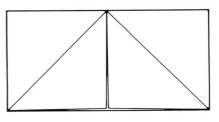

2 *Valley fold the two sides downwards to the centre line. Turn the model over.*

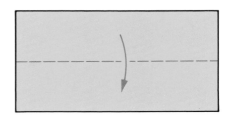

3 *Valley fold in half.*

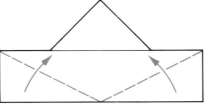

4 *Valley fold the left and right sides upwards as shown. Take care to get the angle right.*

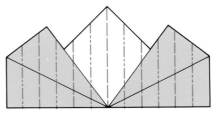

5 *Accordion pleat the whole model. Make sure that one fold passes through the centre line! Press the accordion pleats very firmly then open the model out in a fan shape. Fix the bottom ends of the fan together with a staple or sticky tape and then mount the model onto the lid of your box.*

Wreath

The Crane:

1 *Use a square of paper and start with a bird base (see page 17). Valley fold the left and right sides to the centre line. Repeat behind.*

2 *Inside reverse fold both points as far as they will go.*

3 *Inside reverse fold the head.*

4 *Pull the wings in opposite directions and flatten out the body.*

The Grapes:

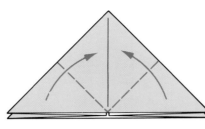
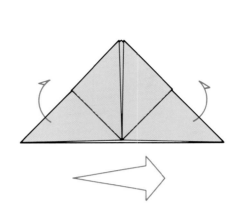
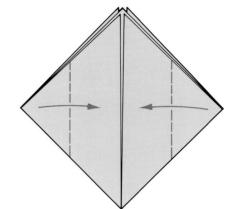

1 *Start with a water bomb base (see page 20). Valley fold the left and right corners upwards to the centre line.*

2 *Mountain fold the other two corners behind.*

3 *Valley fold these two points to the centre line.*

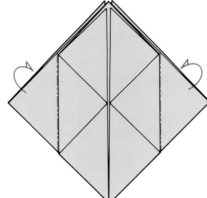
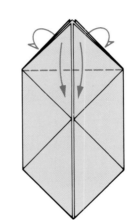

4 *Repeat behind with mountain folds.*

5 *Valley fold these two tips downwards. Repeat behind.*

◀ *This beautiful wreath (see page 27), celebrating nature's abundance at harvest time, uses two completely different models. A thousand cranes strung together are called a sembazuru and it is said that if you manage to make one within any one year of your life you will have great fortune and longevity. The grapes are made from a traditional model, the water bomb.*

6 *Valley fold these two tips again and tuck them into the secret pockets that you will find on closer examination. Repeat behind.*

7 *You will discover a little hole in this position. Blow into this to inflate each grape.*

Wild Goose

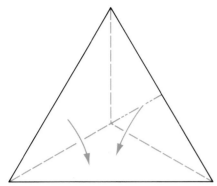

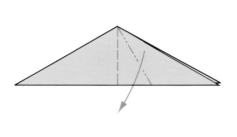

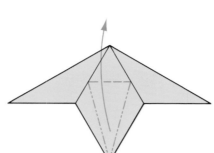

1 *Use an equilateral triangular piece of paper (see page 12). Fold it into a rabbit's ear, following the valley and mountain folds illustrated.*

2 *Lift the right flap into an upright position and squash fold it downwards.*

3 *Petal fold this flap upwards.*

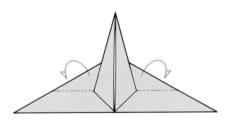

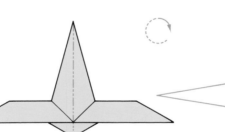

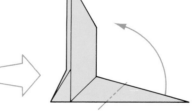

4 *Mountain fold the model as shown to streamline the wings.*

5 *Mountain fold the model in half. Rotate the model 90 degrees.*

6 *Inside reverse fold the neck.*

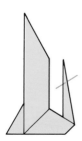

7 *Outside reverse fold the head.*

8 *Valley fold the wings outwards. Fold the beak.*

▶ *The wild goose, butterfly and puppy dog models are all used here to make charming cards (see pages 28–29). Try inventing your own cards using the other animals models in this book.*

Puppy Dog

Use two squares of the same size and colour for this two-piece model.

The Head:

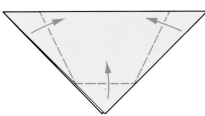

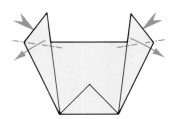

1 *Valley fold the square across the diagonal. Valley fold the nose upwards. Valley fold the ears inwards. Take care to get the angles right.*

2 *Open up and squash fold the ears, applying pressure where shown.*

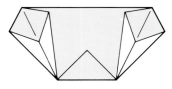

3 *The finished puppy head.*

The Body:

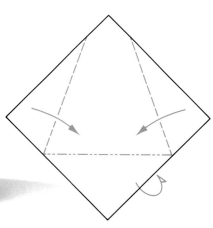

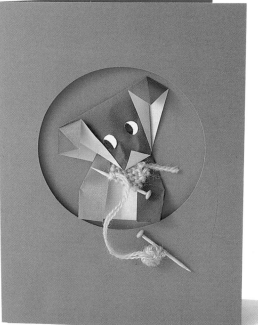

▲ *The expression of this delightful puppy seems to change when the angle of the head is altered. Add a bow tie, a small flower or a tiny piece of knitting to make witty cards for your friends (see page 29).*

4 *Start with the second square in the 'diamond' position. Valley fold the left and right sides inwards. Note that they are not folded to the extreme top point. The long edges that have been folded inwards do not meet the centre line but run parallel to it. Mountain fold the lower section behind.*

5 *Mountain fold the top behind. Sink the two sides with inside reverse folds.*

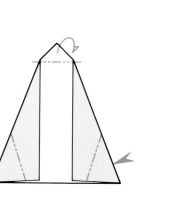

6 *Insert the body into the head and decorate with a nose and eyes.*

Butterfly

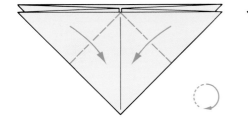

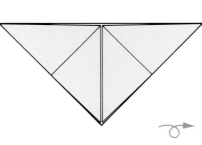

1 *Start with a water bomb base (see page 20). Valley fold down both the flaps to the centre line.*

2 *Turn the model over.*

▼ *A popular subject for the origamian, the butterfly can be combined with beautiful floral motifs to make an elegant, three-dimensional card (see page 28).*

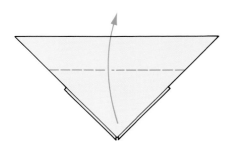

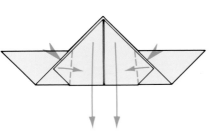

3 *Valley fold the bottom section upwards. Note the proportions! Nearly two thirds.*

4 *Bring both front flaps down. Push in where shown and press flat.*

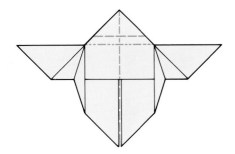

5 *The two folds at the head should be executed in order. The first is a mountain fold at the shoulder and the second a valley fold forward. When you have done that, valley or book fold the butterfly in half.*

6 *Valley fold the wings downwards on both sides.*

93

Paper Play

Here is a selection of projects, hats, puzzles, even jewellery, that will be of especial interest to the younger ones. Even if the first flush of youth has long since deserted you, you will still enjoy folding them.

Hexahexaflexagon
You will need a long strip of quite strong paper. Most good stationery shops sell till rolls and these are perfect for your needs.

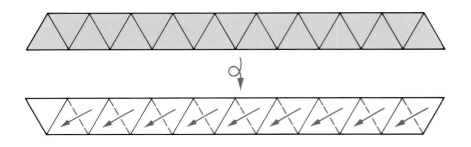

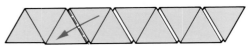

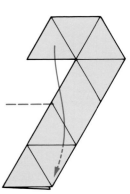

1 *Mark out the strip into 19 equilateral triangles, cutting off the excess paper at either end. Make your triangles as accurate as you possibly can.*

2 *Turn the strip over and mark the triangles on this side. If you now follow the valley folds you will end up with . . .*

3 *. . . a 'flat roll'. Valley fold where shown, bringing the right hand side downwards.*

4 *Valley fold upwards as shown, taking the strip upwards and then tucking it under the blank triangle.*

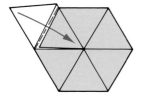

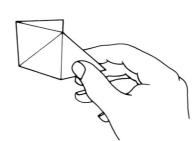

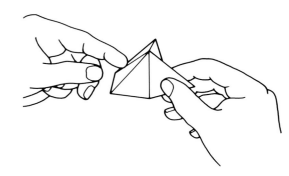

5 *Valley fold the remAining loose triangle inwards and glue onto the triangle below.*

6 *Working the hexahexaflexagon as shown in steps 7–10, paste triangular segments of photographs, six different animals, six famous landmarks or any theme you choose, onto each of the six facets thereby revealed.*

7 *Pinch in adjacent sides together.*

8 *Now push in the opposite side.*

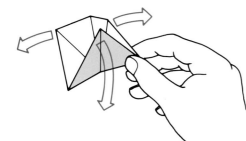

9 *The centre of the model will now open up like the petals of a flower . . .*

10 *. . . until it is flat and reveals a different picture.*

▶ *By repeating the pinching and flexing process, another picture will be revealed. If the model will not open, just pinch a different pair of adjacent sides and you will be off again. Try to find all six illustrations. Be assured that it is possible!*

1

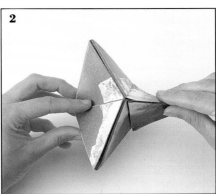

2

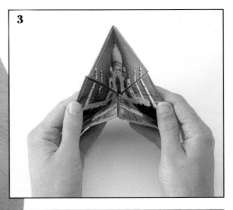

3

4

Valentine

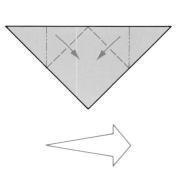

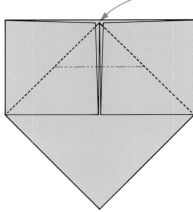

1 *Start with a square folded in half, placing the open ends at the bottom. Mountain fold both corners behind to form a triangle.*

2 *Fold the left corner into an upright position. Open it up and squash fold it into a square shape following the mountain and valley folds illustrated. Repeat with the right corner.*

3 *Reach in and mountain fold the point backwards out of the way.*

▶ *As well as making attractive jewellery for youngsters (see pages 30–31), the valentine also looks wonderful when mounted on a greeting card or used as a gift tag.*

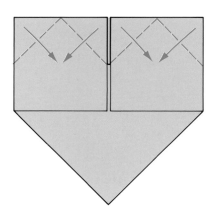

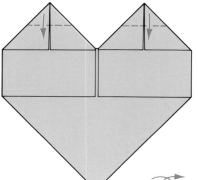

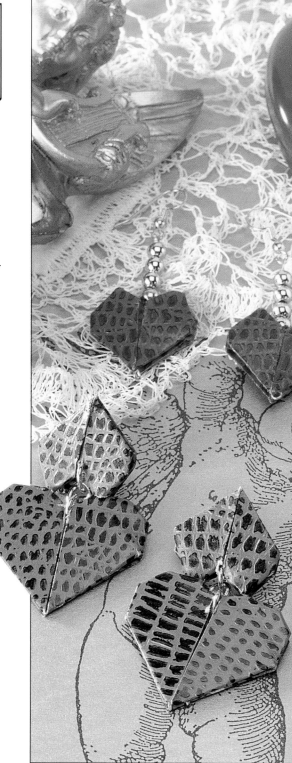

4 *Valley fold the four corners.*

5 *Flatten the tips with little valley folds. Turn the model over.*

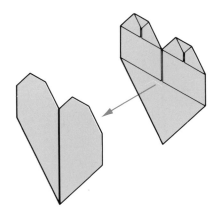

6 *Glue two valentines back to back to make each heart when making the valentine necklace and earrings.*

Japanese Warrior Hat
Use a large piece of paper, at least 76 cm (30 in) square, for this project.

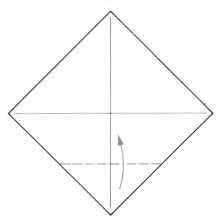

1 *Fold the two diagonals and then open the paper out again. Valley fold the bottom point up to the centre.*

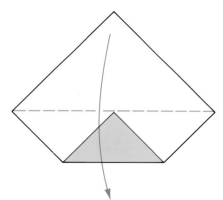

2 *Valley fold the top half downwards.*

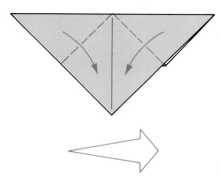

3 *Valley fold the two corners into the centre line.*

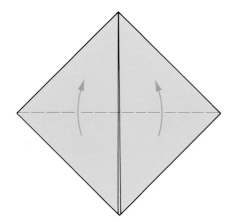

4 Valley fold the two points upwards.

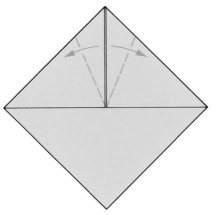

5 Valley fold the two points over left and right to make decorative points.

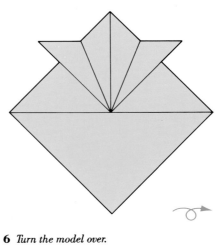

6 Turn the model over.

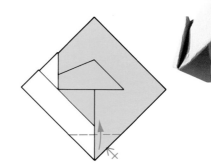

7 Valley fold the bottom point up to touch the centre point.

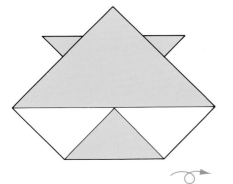

8 Turn the model over again.

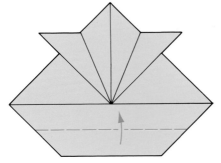

9 Valley fold the bottom section upwards in half, letting the little triangular flap flip out.

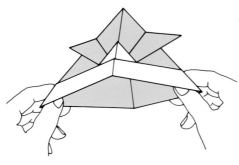

10 Valley fold the bottom section upwards.

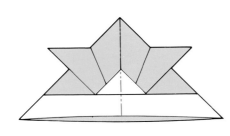

11 Open the helmet up and squash fold it the other way, following the mountain fold illustrated.

12 This shows you how.

13 Valley fold the corners upwards, front and back.

Puppets

Pig and Frog:

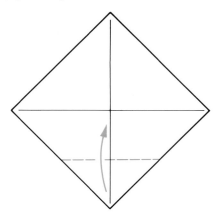

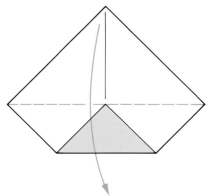

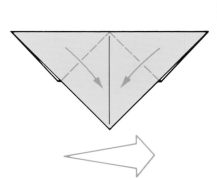

1 *Start with a 30 cm (12 in) square of paper. Pre-crease the two diagonals. Valley fold the bottom point upwards to touch the centre point.*

2 *Valley fold the top half downwards along the centre diagonal.*

3 *Valley fold both sides inwards to the centre vertical line.*

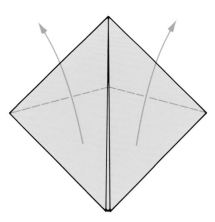

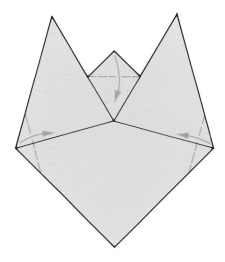

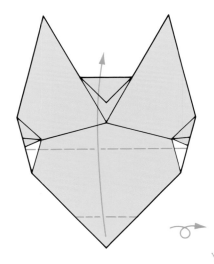

4 *Valley fold both tips upwards (note the slight angle).*

5 *Valley fold the top of the head downwards and the two sides inwards.*

6 *Valley fold the bottom half upwards. Turn the model over.*

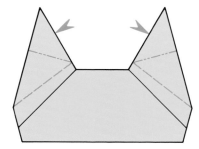

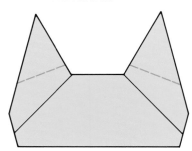

7 *Mountain fold the top of the head inwards. Squash fold the ears as shown for the frog.*

8 *Valley fold the ears towards the face as illustrated for the pig.*

▶ *These simple traditional folds are transformed into lively animal characters by painting on fun faces with poster paints and mounting the puppets on 30 cm (12 in) lengths of bamboo cane or dowelling.*

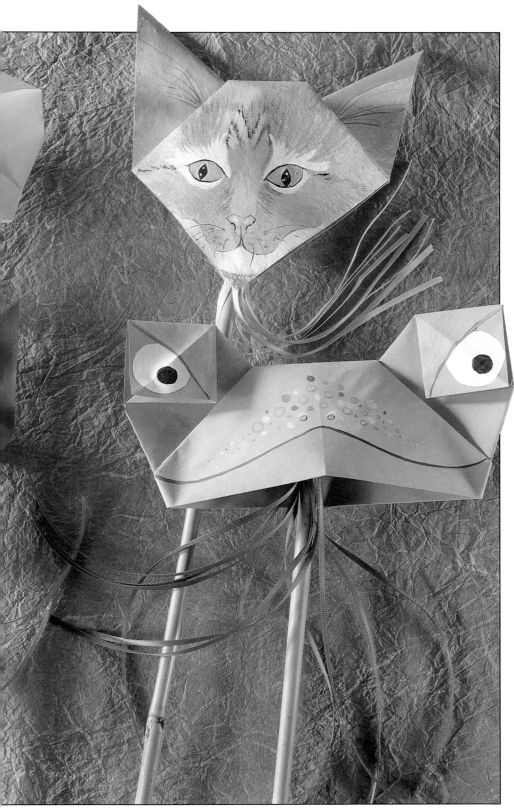

Fox and Cat:

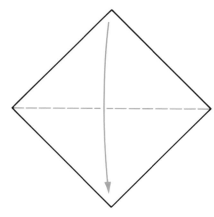

1 *Start with a 30 cm (12 in) square of paper. Valley fold the top half downwards along the centre diagonal.*

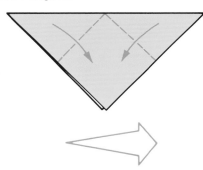

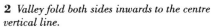

2 *Valley fold both sides inwards to the centre vertical line.*

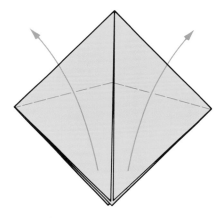

3 *Valley fold both tips upwards (note the slight angle).*

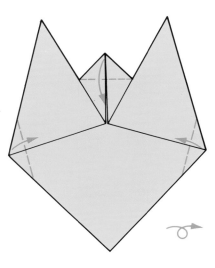

4 *Valley fold the top of the head downwards and the two sides inwards.*

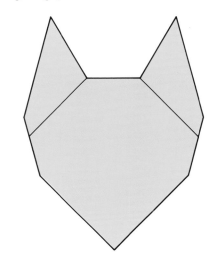

5 *Turn the model over and make up the puppet as suggested opposite.*

Snake in a Box by Jon Tremaine

Fold a traditional box (see pages 50–51) from a 15 cm (6 in) square of paper. Make a shallow lid for it. When the box is formed it will have a 5 x 5 cm (2 x 2 in) interior. To make the snake you must find a 45 x 5 cm (17¾ x 2 in) length of quite thick paper.

1 *Pre-crease all the mountain and valley folds as shown. The last square is left uncreased.*

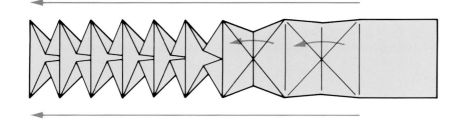

2 *From the left side, follow your folds and let water bomb bases (see page 20) start to form, one on top of the other . . .*

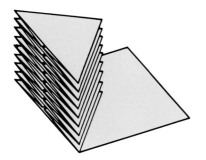

3 *. . . until all eight are formed.*

▶ *This delightful toy is made simply by folding a sequence of water bomb bases. If you cannot find thick paper with an interesting enough pattern, buy white paper and use poster paints or crayons to mimic the texture and colours of snakeskin or to create a jolly snake with coloured dots and stripes.*

104

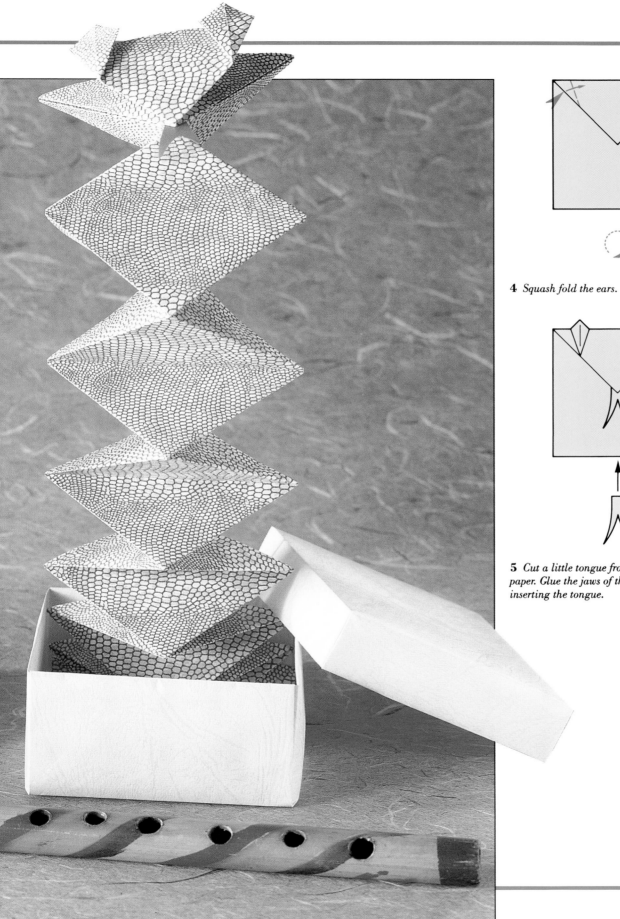

4 *Squash fold the ears.*

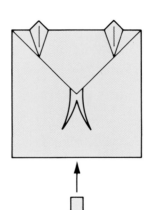

5 *Cut a little tongue from a scrap of red paper. Glue the jaws of the snake together after inserting the tongue.*

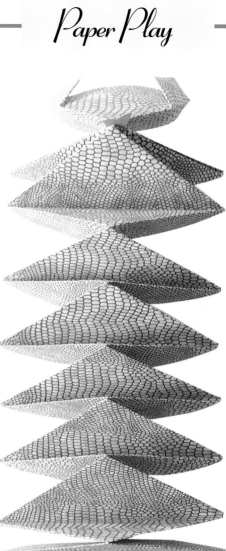

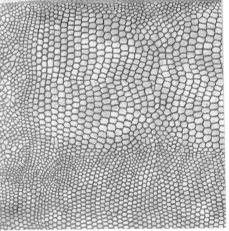

▲ *Pop the snake into the box, squash it down and put on the lid. When the lid is removed, the snake springs up into the air.*

105

Diagrams and Templates

The following two pages present the diagrams needed to reconstruct the pomander and the carrier bag as well as the templates needed for the lily, the tulip and the wild swan card. The diagram for the carrier bag gives **proportional** *measurements to enable you to make a bag of any size and indicates the positioning of the rectangles of stiff card. The templates are same size and should be traced onto a stiff piece of card and cut out.*

POMANDER

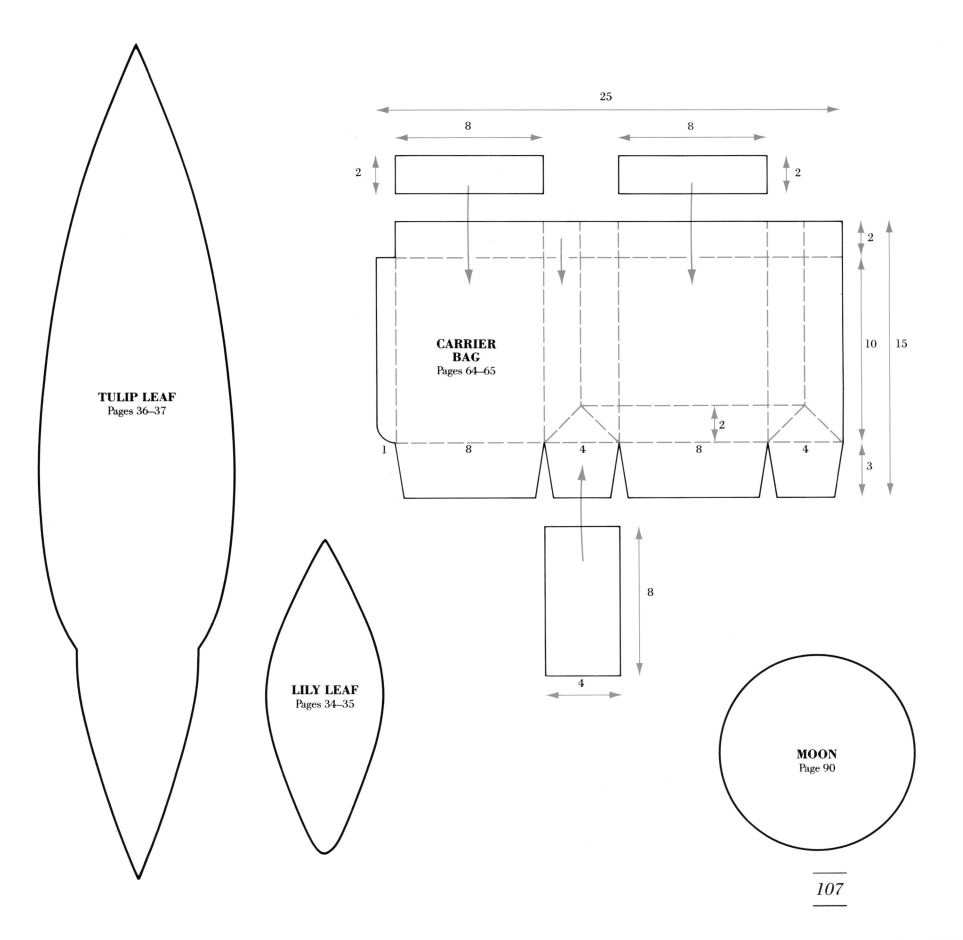

TULIP LEAF
Pages 36–37

LILY LEAF
Pages 34–35

CARRIER BAG
Pages 64–65

MOON
Page 90

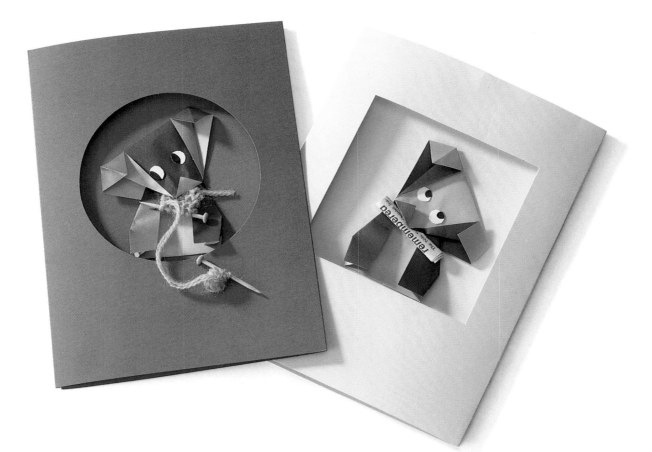

Origami is a wonderful hobby. Meeting and corresponding with other folders around the world is great fun. For this reason, I strongly advise you to make contact with an origami society. They will keep you in touch with the latest publications and help you obtain supplies if you are having difficulties. Here are the addresses of a few societies:

AUSTRALIA
Australian Origami Society
2/5 Broome Street
Highgate
Perth 6000

ENGLAND
British Origami Society
11 Yarningale Road
Kings Heath
Birmingham B14 6LT

JAPAN
Nipon Origami Association
1-0960 Domir Gobancho
12 Gobancho, Chiyodaku
Tokyo 102

UNITED STATES OF AMERICA
The Friends of The Origami Centre of America
15 West 77th Street
New York, NY 10024-5192

CREDITS

Managing Editor: Jo Finnis
Editor: Adèle Hayward
Designer: Jill Coote
Craft Projects and Text: Joanna Jones
Photography: Andrew Dee
Photographic Direction: Nigel Duffield
Illustration: Richard Hawke
Typesetting: SX Composing, Rayleigh, Essex
Production: Ruth Arthur; Sally Connolly;
Neil Randles; Karen Staff; Jonathan Tickner
Director of Production: Gerald Hughes